LESS LAW, MORE ORDER

The Truth about Reducing Crime

IRVIN WALLER

PRAEGER

Westport, Connecticut
London

Library of Congress Cataloging-in-Publication Data

Waller, Irvin.
  Less law, more order : the truth about reducing crime / Irvin Waller.
    p.   cm.
  Includes bibliographical references and index.
  ISBN 0–275–99077–X (alk. paper)
  1. Crime—Government policy—United States.   2. Crime prevention—
  United States.   3. Criminal justice, Administration of—United States. I. Title.
  HV6789.W313   2006
    364.40973—dc22   2006015428

British Library Cataloguing in Publication Data is available.

Library of Congress Catalog Card Number: 2006015428

ISBN: 0–275–99077–X

First published in 2006

Praeger Publishers, 88 Post Road West, Westport, CT 06881
An imprint of Greenwood Publishing Group, Inc.
www.praeger.com

Printed in the United States of America

The paper used in this book complies with the
Permanent Paper Standard issued by the National
Information Standards Organization (Z39.48–1984).

10 9 8 7 6 5 4 3 2 1

Contents

Figures

Acknowledgments

I learned from my father that justice is fighting for what is right. I also learned that the law is an ass. Little did I know at the time, how right he was. He was a lawyer who fought to limit the oppressive powers of the state against underprivileged suspects—undeniably still a noble task. Fighting for the right for people to be safe from crime and the right of young men to be free are noble if forgotten tasks, particularly when supported by so much truth and good sense.

I am grateful for the inspiration that others have given me because they have fought at the pinnacles of their careers for truth in crime policies, prevention of victimization, and investment in young people. I want to mention Gilbert Bonnemaison, Questeur of the French National Assembly; Jack Calhoun, president of the U.S. National Crime Prevention Council; Maria de la Luz Lima, deputy attorney general of Mexico; Dave McCord, executive director of the Canadian Council on Churches and Corrections; Michel Marcus, judge turned European prevention reformer; Irene Melup, a servant for the United Nations; Andrew Rutherford, penal reformer in the United States and United Kingdom; John Stein, victim strategist for the United States; Claude Vézina, Canadian urban safety expert; Brandon Welsh, Canadian truth seeker; Richard Weiler, Canadian social reformer; Nigel Whiskin, British crime reduction advocate; and Marlene Young, U.S. visionary speaker and reformer for victims. Each in their lives and successes showed that prevention is worth fighting for because it avoids trauma and saves lives. Each showed me that truth and good sense must be fought for. Each showed me that one person can make a difference but many can make a bigger difference.

I am grateful to the University of Ottawa and the National Crime Prevention Centre of the Canadian government for providing me with the time to refine some of the material for this book.

I am particularly grateful to my life partner Susan Tanner for supporting my efforts to fight worldwide for this more humane, sensible, and sustainable response to crime.

Irvin Waller
Ottawa, Canada

Introduction:
Truth and Sense, Not Giuliani

Despite significant declines in the last ten years, the Bureau of Justice Statistics (BJS) of the U.S. Department of Justice still recorded an estimated 24 million violent and property victimizations in 2004 in the United States.[1] In 2005, $200 billion of U.S. taxes was spent on 2.5 million employees working in police protection, corrections, and judicial and legal activities.[2] The number of persons incarcerated on an average day topped a record of over 2 million, with another 5 million offenders supervised in the community on probation or parole.[3] In sum, there is still too much crime despite record expenditures.

In contrast, every major organization that has looked at the research, statistics, and good sense on what prevents crime concludes that the rate of victimization in the United States could be much lower without any further increases in police and judges and without so many persons incarcerated or supervised. I will refer to these major organizations as "prestigious" because they are held in wide esteem and trusted for their analysis and recommendations in different areas from engineering to health care. They include names such as the National Research Council (U.S.), the Centers for Disease Control, and the British Audit Commission.[4] Yet when it comes to preventing crime, their recommendations have not yet been put into practice.

I have spent more than thirty years using the truth about crime—research and evidence about its causes and solutions—from this growing body of prestigious organizations to advise ministers of justice or public safety in major countries on every continent. The message that I have brought to them is that they have to care more about victims and victimization and less about punishment if they want to succeed in reducing crime and violence and getting reelected. They need to use what has been demonstrated to work and strategies that focus limited resources at the right time on the risk factors that cause crime and victimization. I have worked closely with many different political elites but my most challenging and rewarding experiences were in South Africa in the Mandela years, England in the Blair years, and Canada in the Trudeau years. Their political elites listened and made incremental changes that would reduce victimization and support victims. Nevertheless, their citizens continue to have the vast majority of their taxes used for the very things that do not work and do not address risk factors—reactive policing, courts, and corrections; that is, the standard system of policing and criminal justice for which there is no or little evidence of effectiveness.

In the United States, the task of getting the political elites to use truth and good sense is particularly challenging as they have increased their spending proportionately so much more than any other affluent country. Further, these expenditures are misspent because they are the opposite of what the prestigious commissions have concluded would save lives and taxes. Compared to countries like Canada or England, the rates of violence in the United States are much worse while ironically the proportion of taxes spent on crime is much higher. It is a policy that allows some disadvantaged young Americans to victimize many Americans before they get incarcerated rather than steer more of those young men away from crime before they could victimize others. Even the poster boy of the world press—Mayor Giuliani—who claimed to have reduced violence dramatically in New York City left New Yorkers two to three times more likely to be murdered than citizens of London or Toronto.

One of the poignant ironies in this is that many of the prestigious organizations and most of the research and truth that they use are based in the United States. Yet that research has been used mostly in other countries such as South Africa, England, and Canada as well as internationally by the United Nations and the World Health Organization. These have come from public health doctors, mayors, and auditors as well as police chiefs, criminologists, and victimologists. They are not based on the legal dogma, jurisprudence, or case law that supports the way taxes have been increased and is a root cause of the failure to reduce victimization.

In the mean time, Americans may not agree on what punishments should be meted out to offenders, but they do believe two to one that more money and effort should go into education and job training than deterring crime by paying for more police, prisons, and judges.[5] In sum, the majority believe that an ounce of prevention is worth a pound of cure, while the prestigious organizations provide scientific confirmation of the same view. So there is a perfect opportunity for the political elites to follow public opinion and spend more of our taxes on what does work to reduce crime rather than continue to misspend it on what is unproven or ineffective.

Unfortunately, serious action to implement these recommendations is long overdue. Occasionally there have been moments of hope when the United States Conference of Mayors or the U.S. National Crime Prevention Council has recognized these recommendations. But they do not have access to legislative reform or the funds to get sustained investment and reform to implement these solutions. Worse, they do not have the attention span to keep advocating for those changes. The political elites need to be more aware of these conclusions as do the voters who elect those elites. So I have written this book so that intelligent readers will be aware of the truth and good sense that would prevent crime and have their taxes spent more judiciously—pun intended. I want readers to know that extensive and sophisticated evidence supports public opinion that sensibly prefers investing more in education and training for youth at risk rather than more police, prisons, and judges. I want more readers to be aware of how less law, more order will protect the most fundamental principle of justice—the right not to be a victim of crime—the right to expect government to use what is known to protect us. I want voters and political elites to know what a serious crime bill would look like that would further reduce victimization in the United States significantly while preventing unwarranted tax increases.

Even in their wildest dreams, after a good meal, our grandparents could not have imagined the comforts so many North Americans and Europeans enjoy today. Many live long and healthy lives, benefit from advanced levels of education and technology, and reap rewards from work and relationships. But our grandparents could not have imagined the persistent rates of crime and victimization that still bedevil us whether rich or poor. During the decades when things were getting rosier for many of us economically, from 1960 to 1980, the rate at which police recorded offenses such as burglary, robbery, and assault was exploding—by some 300 percent. It is true that rates of victimization softened reassuringly in the 1990s, but these reductions still left us today with the risk of victimization at close to double those of the early 1960s—at least according to the FBI.

Tragically, the blight of these crimes, mostly perpetrated by one individual on another, eats away at the pleasure we derive from our health, economic, and educational prosperity. When we are the victims of property offenses such as burglary or car theft, the loss is exacerbated by trauma and anger. When we are the victims of violence such as child abuse, wife battering, or sexual assault, the pleasure and rewards of our intimate relationships are shattered, sometimes permanently. Maybe our grandparents didn't expect so much, because governments did not produce so much in other areas of their life. But we expect governments to husband our taxes and use them effectively to improve our quality of life. Despite crime dropping in the 1990s, there is no other problem area where government is spending more for marginal results than in dealing with crime.

Ironically, we will see that the rate at which we were victimized by these types of crime grew in the 1960s and early 1970s almost in direct proportion to a steady increase in spending on police, judges, and prisoners. When the rate of violent crime dropped in the 1990s dramatically, governments continued to pour even more funds into police, prisons, and judges. The upswing in spending reported by BJS from 1980 to 2001 was massive: a 50 percent increase in the number of police, a 100 percent increase in judicial and legal activities, and a whopping 300 percent increase in the number of people incarcerated and so in expenditures on incarceration.[6] The taxpayers in the United States now pay twice what their British and Canadian counterparts spend and more than what Americans pay for health care.

The spending also accelerated as more knowledge got recognized by these prestigious commissions, and so it was known that there were much better ways to provide quality of life for all and spend our taxes smartly. Much of this research was already known in the 1970s, when I headed up the research and policy group on crime for the Canadian government. Indeed, it had an influence on Canada's decisions to abolish the death penalty, restrict firearms, and engage in research and development on other forms of prevention. But admittedly, the examples were few and far between. However, we began to get more examples as the decades went by. In the 1980s we were able to bring many new examples together for two major international conferences organized by the United States Conference of Mayors and their Canadian and European counterparts. The mayors were impressed by the evidence and the examples so much that they called for a new agenda for safer cities where local governments would be assisted to tackle the social and other risk factors that cause crime in order to stop leaving crime problems only to police, prisons, and judges.

They also called for the establishment of the International Centre for Prevention of Crime (ICPC) to be affiliated with the United Nations as a clearinghouse for the evidence on what prevents and for inspiring examples. It was at the ICPC in the mid-1990s that we used successes from across the world to identify the key ingredients in proven crime reduction strategies and examples of inspiring practices for governments in the United States, Canada, and Europe.[7] A summary of this digest was published by the U.S. Department of Justice to share the extensive data and analysis on the cost-effectiveness of investing in prevention and so confirming the many sayings such as an ounce of prevention is worth a pound of cure. Governments should be sensitive to choosing what is cost-effective rather than continuing what is not. These reports proved to be influential with groups such as the South African Minister of Safety and Security, the Canadian federal government, the British Audit Commission, the Home Office, and the most prestigious British government agency—The Treasury. The Audit Commission extended this analysis for England and Wales to show how taxes spent on policing, courts, and prisons to tackle youth offending were "misspent"—a key concept for this book.[8]

However, research did not stand still in the 1990s. More evidence was accumulating about what actions work to reduce victimization in the United States and England and Wales but also in The Netherlands, Australia, and other similar countries. The ICPC added this to its second major publication, including important sources in other languages than English. It contributed to the work of the U.S. National Commission on Criminal Justice in 1995.[9] In 1996, the Centers for Disease Control gave important recognition to the importance of preventing violence by providing funding to a program led by Del Elliott to identify "Blue Prints" of what works to prevent violence. Shortly after, the Office for Juvenile Justice and Delinquency Prevention of the U.S. Department of Justice offered funding which would be used to replicate these Blue Prints in other locations in the United States.[10] Also in 1996, the National Institute of Justice of the U.S. Department of Justice funded a team of criminologists at the University of Maryland led by Lawrence Sherman to bring together the results of the evaluations of the effectiveness of the expenditures by the U.S. government on reducing victimization—first published as *What Works, What Doesn't and What Is Promising.*[11]

These were all important in providing a base for a more effective, cost-effective, and youth-friendly vision as to what was the truth about what works to prevent crime. Then the prestigious U.S. National Research Council started to reexamine these same issues—often going into more depth and using even more up-to-date material. I have been particularly impressed by the report that included seminal work on the effectiveness of policing but they also looked at family violence, juvenile offending, school violence, and drugs.[12]

This movement occurred not just in Canada, England, and the United States but internationally. The same knowledge from many of the same studies was consolidated, verified, and publicized by public health doctors and others working with the World Health Organization in their encyclopedic and seminal world reports on violence and health as well as on traffic fatalities.[13] It has given birth to a group called the Campbell Collaboration to oversee reviews of the highest quality research on the effects of criminological interventions for the future. Brandon Welsh and David Farrington have just published the first collection of these reviews.[14]

The conclusions from these prestigious commissions are clear that limiting our response to the "standard" use of police, courts, and corrections is not the way to prevent and reduce these crimes. "Standard" is used by the National Research Council (U.S.) to refer to most local police agencies that are wasting nearly 65 percent of our taxes to respond to 911 calls, most of which are neither urgent nor likely to lead to the arrest of a suspect.[15] I will extend the term standard to include lawyers and judges defending the rights of accused persons while trampling on or forgetting basic principles of justice for victims. Standard means misspending significant amounts of our taxes to incarcerate young adults, who are disproportionately African American or Hispanic in the United States, black in the United Kingdom, and Aboriginal in Canada.

Standard means correctional programs in the 1970s that had shown not to prevent reoffending as research has shown ever since.[16]

The political elites assume that the more we pay for law enforcement after the victimization, the more we will get "order"—safer homes, schools, streets, and communities. But the equation that emerges from the prestigious commissions is that the less we pay for standard law enforcement and the more we invest in focused prevention, the more we will get order. This equation is *Less Law, More Order*. When we invest in solving problems by tackling the risk factors that cause crime, we get less crime. We have to stop a political reaction to crime, that is, more punishment and police, and replace it with a political strategy, that is, more prevention and smarter use of policing to solve the risk factors that cause crime.

The authors of these prestigious scientific and government bodies would wring their hands—and so should we—as they see massive resources diverted from the very services that prevent crime cost-effectively to law and order that does not. That is, our taxes are used for more police and prisons instead of more public health nurses, youth workers, college teachers, job trainers, and so on. This is not a general plea for a utopian world of perfect social welfare programming. It is a hard-nosed conclusion that victimization would be reduced significantly by hiring those workers to deliver their services to those young adults, families, and neighborhoods that are most at risk—often those who are not just poor but also discriminated against because of their racial characteristics. We do not need more police, but more intelligent use of the police we have. If we did this, we would need fewer judges and have many fewer prisoners. More importantly, we would have fewer victims hurt by crime.

Many newspaper readers would question this equation of less law, more order. After all, they have been led to believe that crime was forced down in New York City because Mayor Rudy Giuliani spent a lot more on law and order and demanded tougher policing practices. Yes, there was a significant drop in crime in New York City during the 1990s. Yes, he did spend a lot more on law and order and encouraged tougher policing methods. But no, most of the drop was not due to Giuliani or being tough on petty offenses or clearing up garbage. Giuliani was in the right place at the right time because crime rates crashed across the United States in the 1990s. In fact they had already dropped significantly in the four years before Giuliani was even elected.

These beliefs that more police and tougher policies are the reason for the crime drop are widespread. I advise governments around the world and before I do they have already made up their mind that more and tougher police will solve their violence problem. How could so few newspaper editors bamboozle so many intelligent readers? Disappointingly, Giuliani's claims have been repeated by the world's media and believed by the world's politicians. As Franklin Zimring reminded us thirty years ago, spin masters can make us believe that politicians' actions caused a trend when in reality their election just coincided with a trend already in place.[17]

Nevertheless, it is true that when the New York City Police Department went after perpetrators of small crimes, the police ended up stopping persons whom they checked for outstanding warrants, handguns, and drugs, and so they were getting handguns out of the wrong hands and nabbing some criminals wanted for much more serious crimes. These "problem-oriented" or what I call smart policies may have had some impact. In Chapter 5, we will look at whether Giuliani did make a contribution over and above the national crime drop.

Even so, any success that Giuliani achieved came disturbingly at the expense of taxpayers and continued increases in the numbers of young men behind bars—what I call hyperincarceration. Such policies continue the use of incarceration, particularly for the classic oppressed racial groups. More than 2 million persons are behind bars in the United States today—22 percent of all persons incarcerated in the world—a rate per 100,000 higher than any other nation.[18] These policies both increase taxes and take resources away from programs that are known—as *Less Law, More Order* will show—to be more effective in reducing crime at less human and financial cost. These policies do not provide positive futures for the persons—mostly young men—who bear the brunt of being behind bars.

The charisma and public relations machine of Giuliani is one thing but wacky ideas are another. Even when it is reported in *Freakonomics*, some politicians buy the argument (and the book) that an abortion decision by the U.S. Supreme Court was the cause of the same dramatic drop for which Giuliani had already claimed paternity—pun intended! We will see that the trends in rates of crime bear little resemblance to what would be expected as a result of a Supreme Court decision in the mid-1980s.

But this book is not just about preventing crime and victimization; it is also about ensuring justice and support for the victims of crime. Yes, preventing victimization should be a basic right for victims. But when policies fail to eliminate crime, the political elites need to put in place services to meet the needs of those victims. Also they must ensure that the cooperation of victims with the police, courts, and corrections industry does not make the trauma of victims worse. They need to guarantee that victims can get restitution, protect their safety, seek truth, and look after their legitimate interests within the criminal justice system.

These concerns for support and justice for victims are still not given the priority they deserve by politicians. The prestigious commissions in the United States, as in other countries like England and Canada, overlook victims. The World Health Organization is an exception in its efforts to reduce violence and fatalities on the road aimed at reducing victimization directly. Their public health doctors included many recommendations to assist victims of violence. Fortunately as early as 1982, the U.S. President's Task Force on Victims of Crime made comprehensive and impressive recommendations that were more extensive and fundamental than any report in any other country.[19] The chair of that task force in the name of the U.S. government actively supported the adoption by the United Nations of the set of basic principles of justice for victims in 1985.[20] Yes, the United States has done more than any other country to meet those rights, principally through the 1984 Victims of Crime Act. It has also done more to assess how these can be improved. In 1998, the U.S. Department of Justice's Office for Victims of Crime did its own evaluation of what still needs to be done, which we will use in Chapter 6.[21]

It is increasingly recognized by those working with victims that people like you or me who may have suffered loss, injury, and trauma at the hands of an offender are often further traumatized by the police, lawyers, and judges who ignore the needs of victims whether in their zeal for law and order or justice for offenders. If you become a witness in the prosecution of the offense against you, you will find out quickly that it is the law and order's process, not yours. You will be required to testify at a time and in a manner that pays little attention to your trauma, fears, or frustration. Even if the court considers seriously reparation from the offender, you will be lucky to have this paid to you.

"Bills of rights" across North America set out guidelines so that victims will ostensibly get information, support, reparation, and representation, but in most cases they are just a "bill of goods" as the rights are not respected and cannot be enforced. In the U.S. Senate in 2004, a bipartisan motion supported by President Clinton and President Bush could not garner the sixty-seven votes needed to amend the constitution to recognize these rights—ironically, the resistance came from senators with a human rights education but that education is blind to human rights for victims.

"Populist" politicians leave the impression that law and order—more police, courts, and corrections—is what is demanded by victims of crime. Some victims do want harsher punishment for the offender, while others do not. All victims, however, want more protection, recognition, and consideration. Victims want to be sure that they will not be victims again and that they will be treated with respect by the criminal justice system, which to them is just a system of justice for criminals, a system blind to the basic rights of victims. They want less law but more attention to their needs—more order for them.

With a few recent exceptions, governments enact criminal justice legislation for both adults and juveniles without regard to what is likely to be effective in reducing offending. They engage in a curious calculus that is irrelevant to preventing victimization of how much a given responsibility is worth in time behind bars. At election time, they propose even heavier penalties and minimum sentences without any care for what these will cost to taxpayers and offenders or what little difference they will make to reducing victimization.

Somehow they assume that enacting a penalty and empowering courts to impose it will reduce crime. Nothing is further from reality and it must change. In fact if deterrence worked, there would not have been the rapid increases that led to 2 million persons incarcerated in the United States, because they would have been deterred from crime. This book casts into doubt the effectiveness of the standard roles of police, prosecutors, and judges as well as the cost-effectiveness and hence the utility of incarcerating large numbers of common offenders. The information and conclusions of *Less Law, More Order* are controversial, questioning this obsession with the antiquated concept of free will that underpins our modern criminal justice system.

But why write about crime and violence when terrorism seems to be the major challenge facing the world. It was a tragedy when nearly 3,000 people died and many more were injured and traumatized in the horrific catastrophes on September 11, 2001. The mayhem that occurred within just a few hours on one day must be faced, but every year just in the United States five times that number are murdered and five times that number are killed in drunk-driver crashes. Common crime and violence is still way more likely to hit your family than terrorism. These deaths like most interpersonal violence are preventable if we acted on the truth and good sense presented in this book. So while it is important to act to prevent terrorism, it is important to act to prevent violence. Further, if we can stop crime and violence by applying what is known to work, it would free police and safety personnel from reacting to crime to fight terrorists.

Some argue that it is time to concentrate on white-collar crime—to get heavier penalties used for the rich who abuse their powers to defraud thousands of victims of their life savings. *Less Law, More Order* questions whether criminal penalties are a cost-effective solution to common violent and property crime. I am sure that the solutions to white-collar crime are not to substitute the rich and powerful for the poor and disadvantaged behind bars. Yes, it is an important form of victimization by crime, but one that others must address.

Regardless, the central issues in the book are how to use our taxes to reduce the persistent problem of victimization by interpersonal crime. I cut through the theoretical and statistical jargon of so many of these scientific reports to present compelling evidence accumulated over the past twenty years. Yes, it tells truths that sometimes are obvious. But these prestigious commissions arrived at these truths after looking carefully at hundreds of scientific studies completed in the last thirty years. I have used their conclusions in Chapter 1 to piece together an indictment of the costly failures and extraordinarily expensive successes of "standard" ways to use police, courts, and corrections—responding to 911 calls when they cannot make a difference, paying for lawyers and judges who ignore victims, incarcerating young adults who should be at school and working to pay taxes.

Less Law, More Order starts with what is wrong but it is mostly about how to put it right. It empowers the reader to know what reduces the number of victims, how victims can get justice, and what to demand from government to ensure changes are made. Chapter 2 shows the significant positive effect of policies and programs that keep kids at risk in school and the community, instead of putting them behind bars. Chapter 3 shows how action to outlaw violence in our homes, on our roads, and on our streets prevents victimization more than law and order does. That is why we need to control better the volatile mix of violence in homes, handguns, alcohol, and drugs. Chapter 4 examines how our close neighbors can help us better watch out for ourselves and our property as well as how alarms and private security can do the same for those who can afford them. However, I call for caution with overreliance on these, particularly as they can backfire. Chapter 5 turns to an analysis of how law enforcement and police can prevent crime, including an assessment of the research on their impact in New York City, Boston, and Chicago. I look at whether police matter to victims of crime as much as the proponents of 911 would make us think. Chapter 6 focuses on what works to treat victims of crime fairly, how law and order needs them, and how giving standing to them in criminal courts would protect their rights to restitution, personal safety, and truth.

These chapters each conclude that a shift from more law and order to less law, more order is needed to reduce victimization, husband our taxes, and treat victims and young adults fairly. Chapter 7 explains why cities are the thin line that will protect us and our pocket books. I look at what mayors called for ten years ago, how funds went elsewhere, and how other countries have got ahead of us. In Chapter 8, I focus on the strategies that politicians can adopt to make the shift from too much law and order to less law, more order. I call for a permanent Office for Crime Prevention at the top levels of every order of government to diagnose the problems, plan and implement solutions, and demonstrate whether these are more cost-effective than the standard approaches.

In *Less Law, More Order*, it is demonstrated how affordable government policies can protect the most basic right of citizens to have their life, liberty, and property protected. I make and back up the claim that proven crime prevention and reduction policies can help us cut rates of victimization significantly while investing in positive futures for our youth at risk and avoiding wasted taxes. On the basis of the evaluations of projects, a further 50 percent reduction in both property and violent crime is achievable if socioeconomic trends stay steady. Smart action by our political elites will save many lives wasted by trauma and misguided justice, avoid any increased tax burden in the name of public safety, and encourage better futures for young men at risk.

Abbreviations

Audit Commission: Audit Commission for Local Authorities and National Health Service in England and Wales.

BJS: Bureau of Justice Statistics, part of the U.S. Department of Justice.

CCTV: Closed circuit television, a technology used particularly in England and Wales to provide surveillance in private and public areas.

CDC: Centers for Disease Control, part of the U.S. Department of Health and Human Services located in Atlanta. It refers mainly here to the Division of Violence Prevention, which is in the National Center for Injury Prevention and Control.

Compstat: A computerized system for analyzing police statistics and holding police commanders accountable, originally developed for the New York City Police Department.

CPTED: Crime Prevention through Environmental Design, a concept similar to situational crime prevention that became popular in the 1980s and resulted in modifications of designs of buildings, parking lots, and cities.

FBI: The Federal Bureau of Investigation is the principal investigative arm of the United States Department of Justice. It reports annually on crime as recorded by police departments.

FCM: The Federation of Canadian Municipalities is the national voice of municipal government in Canada.

Gaçaça: A Rwandan word that refers to a community justice process established by law to report the truth of what happened in killings and rapes during the genocide in 1994.

HMIC: Her Majesty's Inspectorate of Constabulary is an agency of the Home Office of England and Wales, which employs distinguished police chiefs to assess the quality of British police services. The Home Office provides funding to police services, conditional on the HMIC approving the quality of services.

IACP: International Association of Chiefs of Police is the world's largest nonprofit association of police executives with 17,000 members, headquartered near Washington, D.C.

IBCR: International Bureau for Children's Rights, based in Montreal.

ICPC: The International Centre for Prevention of Crime, affiliated with the United Nations, shares knowledge of what works to prevent crime.

LEAA: Law Enforcement Assistance Administration.

National Research Council (U.S.): The National Research Council is part of the National Academies that enlist the foremost scientists in the United States to provide policy advice under a congressional charter.

NOVA: National Organization for Victim Assistance promotes rights and services for victims of crime and other crises.

NYPD: New York Police Department, the municipal police service for New York City.

OVC: Office for Victims of Crime in the U.S. Department of Justice.

RCT: Randomized controlled trial refers to a scientific test to evaluate whether an innovation such as preventing dropouts is better at reducing the likelihood of arrest than the standard response. It is a field experiment where the subjects are assigned at random to an innovation or a comparison group so that the different outcomes can only be due to the innovation.

SAMHSA: Substance Abuse and Mental Health Services Administration, part of U.S. Department of Health and Human Services.

UCR: Uniform Crime Report, the national report issued by the FBI on crime recorded by police departments.

USCM: The United States Conference of Mayors is a national nonpartisan organization representing cities, which lobbies for improved solutions to urban problems.

VOCA: Victims of Crime Act, 1984.

WHO: World Health Organization.

WSIPP: Washington State Institute for Public Policy.

WSV: World Society of Victimology.

YIP: Youth Inclusion Programme, a successful program of the U.K. Youth Justice Board.

YJB: Youth Justice Board, established by the 1998 Crime and Disorder Act in England and Wales.

So let us look at whether being tough on crime is effective in reducing crime. We will start by looking at the real risks of crime to us as members of the public, and then at what crime costs us as victims and taxpayers, the phenomenon of victimizing the victims, the search for the causes of and solutions to crime, and what really does affect crime rates.

CRIME IS TOUGH ON MANY

Imagine eight average families in the United States, the United Kingdom, or Canada. Each year, one of these families will call the police because they reported being the victims of a burglary, car theft, assault, or other common crime. The national rates of crime are surprisingly similar in Western Europe and North America for everything except for violence with a handgun—where the United States is still the unfortunate champion.

According to police statistics reported by the Federal Bureau of Investigation (FBI) for the United States, the average risk of a citizen being victimized by a common crime in 2004 was at least twice the figure in 1962. Yes, rates of crime declined relative to the population in the 1990s, but this was not enough to offset the steady and cumulatively large increases that occurred in the 1960s and 1970s.

Those who have not been victims of crime are quick to question these statistics. They say that it has not happened to them and the people they know, so how could the rate be so high? But unfortunately, they are wrong. Public statistical agencies such as the FBI confirm these rates, using statistics reported to them by local police services.

In fact, the situation is much worse because many victims do not report their victimization to the police. The Bureau of Justice Statistics (BJS) of the U.S. Department of Justice undertakes large-scale scientific surveys to measure the rate at which adults become victims of crime. One such survey is known as the National Crime Victimization Survey. These surveys are made independent of police and so are not affected by police decisions to make their statistics look better—or worse. The surveys are conducted independently of police decisions to allocate more or less resources to detectives or response to 911 calls. The surveys go directly to adults in households in the same way as the census or annual surveys on unemployment. Indeed the Census Bureau identifies the representative sample and administers the survey for the U.S. Department of Justice.

These surveys measure rates of victimization by common offenses such as residential burglary, car theft, assault, robbery, and sexual assault. These surveys have been done every year since 1972—that is, for more than thirty years. They are done on an impressive scale. In 2004, in the United States, nearly 150,000 individuals aged 12 and older were interviewed in 84,000 households. Similar surveys are now commonplace in other industrialized countries. For instance, the British Crime Victim Survey is conducted annually on a

VOCA: Victims of Crime Act, 1984.

WHO: World Health Organization.

WSIPP: Washington State Institute for Public Policy.

WSV: World Society of Victimology.

YIP: Youth Inclusion Programme, a successful program of the U.K. Youth Justice Board.

YJB: Youth Justice Board, established by the 1998 Crime and Disorder Act in England and Wales.

1

Tough on Crime Is Tough on Us

Many of us react to a news report of a sensational and exceptional crime with frustration and a reflexive cry of "Punish the criminals!" When we read the newspaper headline about the latest sensational crime, our reaction is "Punish them harder!" We believe that catching, convicting, and incarcerating offenders will adequately punish the wrongdoers and—somehow—protect us from harm, a belief reinforced by law-and-order shows on televisions, Rambo-type police on our theater screens, and crime coverage in our newspapers. Worse, this belief is reinforced by political elites at election time as they abandon reason in an attempt to out do one another promising more police and punishments rather than less crime and taxes.

Whatever the seductive make-believe of Hollywood, the reality is quite otherwise. As this book will demonstrate, getting tough on crime in most cases has not led, and will not lead, to significant reductions in crime except at enormous cost to taxpayers or cutbacks in the social programs that would reduce crime more effectively. So we find ourselves in a bind. First, crime-busting policies cost us more in taxes, as governments at all levels hire more police, make work for lawyers, and pay for more incarceration. Second, these spendthrift policies and programs have little effect in preventing crime or deterring crooks, let alone rehabilitating offenders or teaching criminals a lesson. Third, in this process, the basic principles of justice for crime victims are trampled by police wanting to catch offenders, prosecutors wanting evidence, and judges wanting decisions. This is magnified by reporters and broadcasters wanting headlines.

So let us look at whether being tough on crime is effective in reducing crime. We will start by looking at the real risks of crime to us as members of the public, and then at what crime costs us as victims and taxpayers, the phenomenon of victimizing the victims, the search for the causes of and solutions to crime, and what really does affect crime rates.

CRIME IS TOUGH ON MANY

Imagine eight average families in the United States, the United Kingdom, or Canada. Each year, one of these families will call the police because they reported being the victims of a burglary, car theft, assault, or other common crime. The national rates of crime are surprisingly similar in Western Europe and North America for everything except for violence with a handgun—where the United States is still the unfortunate champion.

According to police statistics reported by the Federal Bureau of Investigation (FBI) for the United States, the average risk of a citizen being victimized by a common crime in 2004 was at least twice the figure in 1962. Yes, rates of crime declined relative to the population in the 1990s, but this was not enough to offset the steady and cumulatively large increases that occurred in the 1960s and 1970s.

Those who have not been victims of crime are quick to question these statistics. They say that it has not happened to them and the people they know, so how could the rate be so high? But unfortunately, they are wrong. Public statistical agencies such as the FBI confirm these rates, using statistics reported to them by local police services.

In fact, the situation is much worse because many victims do not report their victimization to the police. The Bureau of Justice Statistics (BJS) of the U.S. Department of Justice undertakes large-scale scientific surveys to measure the rate at which adults become victims of crime. One such survey is known as the National Crime Victimization Survey. These surveys are made independent of police and so are not affected by police decisions to make their statistics look better—or worse. The surveys are conducted independently of police decisions to allocate more or less resources to detectives or response to 911 calls. The surveys go directly to adults in households in the same way as the census or annual surveys on unemployment. Indeed the Census Bureau identifies the representative sample and administers the survey for the U.S. Department of Justice.

These surveys measure rates of victimization by common offenses such as residential burglary, car theft, assault, robbery, and sexual assault. These surveys have been done every year since 1972—that is, for more than thirty years. They are done on an impressive scale. In 2004, in the United States, nearly 150,000 individuals aged 12 and older were interviewed in 84,000 households. Similar surveys are now commonplace in other industrialized countries. For instance, the British Crime Victim Survey is conducted annually on a

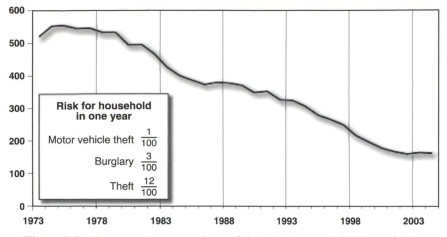

Figure 1.1. Property crime rates: Rate of victimization per 1,000 households.

sample of 60,000 households and has become the benchmark for measuring the success of British crime reduction strategies. Canada is behind the others as it undertakes its survey only every five years and on a comparatively small sample of 25,000 households. However, Canada has pioneered a similar survey to measure violence against women, which is beginning to be taken up in other countries. There is also an international crime victim survey that enables a comparison of rates between different countries.

These surveys confirm that victimization is much more common than the police know. The bad news is that the real rate of victimization is nearly double that of the rate known to the police. You only need to imagine four families—not eight—in your neighborhood to find one that has been a victim of a common offense. The good news is that the rate of both violent and property crimes in the United States has never been lower since 1972. As shown in a graph from the BJS (see Figure 1.1), the rate of property crime has dropped steadily from one in every two households in 1972 to one in four households in 2003. This decline is partly the result of the decline in the proportion of teenage and young adult males in the population. But even with this drop, there are an estimated 24 million victimizations for approximately 105 million households—that is one in every four households. This includes one motor vehicle theft and three residential burglaries every year for every 100 households.

As shown by another graph from the BJS (see Figure 1.2), the trend in the rate of violent victimization did not drop dramatically from a rate of one in twenty until 1994 when it fell rapidly to one in fifty. But even with this drop, there is one sexual assault, two assaults with injury, and two robberies for every 1,000 persons of age 12 and older. The timing of the start of the

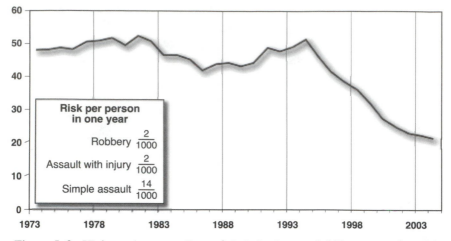

Figure 1.2. Violent crime rates: Rate of victimization per 1,000 persons of age 12 or older.

decline coincided with the election of Giuliani in New York. In other words, this significant drop in crime in New York City was part of a national decline, not something specially engineered by Giuliani.

Nationally, there are about six murders per 100,000 persons—proportionately the same as the rate for New York City. These rates are much higher than those found in Canada or Western Europe. So, the much higher expenditures on policing and staggeringly high rates of incarceration are not enough to lower murder rates to those of Europe or Canada. In addition, several more persons are killed in crimes that did not involve deliberate killing—manslaughters. There are also more persons killed in traffic accidents involving drunk or dangerous drivers than those murdered or victims of manslaughter.

These surveys undertaken by the Bureau of the Census are also sobering for those who advocate law and order because they show the widespread lack of use of the police by victims. During 2004, 50 percent of all violent victimizations and 61 percent of property victimizations were not reported to the police. Imagine if half the patients who are sick did not go to doctors. In Canada and England it is worse, as fewer victims decide to report as the years go by. If you are insured, you have to report your car as stolen in order to claim your insurance. If your house is broken into, you make a judgment as to whether the loss justifies a claim on your insurance. If you decide to make a claim, then you must report the offense to the police. However, if you are the victim of an assault by a family member within your home or of a sexual assault, you will hesitate to report it to the police for many different reasons.

These surveys also show that some families will be repeat victims—that is, some of them will be victims more than once in the year being surveyed. Some 40 percent of assault victims will be assaulted a second time within a year. More than 10 percent of car theft and burglary victims are victimized again in the same time period. Women are particularly at risk of violence in their intimate relationships; much of this crime is repeated and never comes to the attention of the police. Although less than 3 percent of women are assaulted—battered—by an intimate partner in a year, many are assaulted several times in a year by the same partner. Cumulatively in their lifetime, more than 25 percent of women are assaulted in an intimate relationship.

But these surveys focus only on those over age 12. It is much harder to get reliable statistics on the victimization of children. Childcare authorities confirm that more than one child in seven is abused; the Child Welfare League confirms that in the United States alone, at least 900,000 children are determined to be victims of maltreatment, often perpetrated by their parents or caregivers. Of these, 1,200 are murdered. Child abuse is well established as an experience that increases the likelihood of the children themselves becoming violent in their teen and adult years.

But this is just in the home. Surveys in the United States estimate that one in fourteen schoolchildren are bullied each year, though there are no ideal large-scale surveys. These are probably underestimates as large-scale surveys of 25,000 children in schools in Canada, undertaken by the national statistical agency, show that one in twenty boys and one in fourteen girls are bullied in school. Not only is bullying unpleasant for the victim but it is one of the factors thought to precipitate violence in later life, and certainly a key factor in high-profile school shootings such as in Columbine.

TOUGH ON VICTIMS

For too long, these statistics have been interpreted as the rate at which criminals commit offenses. Indeed, the law enforcement and criminal justice complex focus on justice for the criminal rather than justice for the broader community and the victim. But these statistics also represent the rate at which people—you and I—suffer loss, harm, and trauma. When a burglar enters a home, the resident may lose a television or a computer, but the victim also loses the feeling that home is a safe place. The damage done to the home is often experienced as a violation of the person. If we are the victims of a crime, we will likely suffer loss and feel shock and anger. Loss resulting from crime is a lot more than merely the financial loss, say, of a television, bicycle, or valuable personal property. The victim incurs many other losses, because the property had sentimental value as a heirloom or photographic memories of happy days, or the offense destroyed the victim's sense of confidence. The impact of a violent crime goes way beyond the immediate physical injury, because the crime produces a psychological trauma, now recognized as post-traumatic stress disorder in the *Diagnostic Statistical Manual of Mental Health Disorders* of the American Psychiatric Association.

In only about half the cases, we as victims will not call the police, but if we do, the experience may make matters worse. Unfortunately, it is not till after we have called the police that we discover that they are unlikely to identify an offender unless we can provide them with the details. And in the statistically unlikely event that there is a prosecution in the name of the state, matters worsen as we learn firsthand that the crime-busting system is organized around the police officers, judges, and lawyers. We—the victims of the offense and often thought to be the reason for the investigation—have no representation to protect our safety, get the truth or restitution, or even just express our concerns. In the extreme, we may even be punished if we do not come to court when the judge requires—even if our appearance would put our life in danger or cause us major inconvenience or loss of our income. The judges may ask us to talk about the victimization without any concern for the emotional consequences of our reliving the trauma of the crime. Judges and lawyers may be aggressive in asking questions in court that unnecessarily traumatize us.

In 1982, I started an initiative with a new international nongovernment organization—the World Society of Victimology—to change this. In 1979, I was elected to the board of the National Organization for Victim Assistance (NOVA) in the United States. NOVA was already advocating successfully for reforms in many different states. Legislation had been adopted in states such as Wisconsin, California, and New York to identify rights for victims of crime. So I got together a small group from different countries to develop a proposal to the United Nations to decide the basic principles of justice for victims of crime. After three whirlwind years of negotiations with different government and nongovernment organizations, the U.N. General Assembly adopted a resolution, adopting the Declaration of Basic Principles of Justice for Victims of Crime and Abuse of Power. This declaration recognizes the harm that is done to victims and their families by crime and sets out principles of justice for the victim who must get information and services from police, health, and others as well as restitution from the offender, reparation from the state, and a right to defend their personal interests.

The United States is traditionally reticent to encourage U.N. standards. However, in 1982, Lois Haight Herrington—an articulate California prosecutor—was nominated as the chair of the U.S. President's Task Force on Victims of Crime. Her task force produced sixty-eight recommendations to correct what she saw as the appalling lack of balance in the U.S. system of law enforcement and criminal justice. Her report was quickly followed in 1984 by a federal legislation called the Victims of Crime Act, which established a high-level Office for Victims of Crime in the U.S. Department of Justice and was enabled to use federal fines to fund its activities. She was appointed as the first director of that office.

In 1985, she came to the U.N. meeting in Milan, Italy, to discuss the proposed U.N. declaration and on behalf of the U.S. government gave a charismatic speech that settled the need to adopt the declaration. Shortly thereafter, the U.N. General Assembly adopted the Declaration on Basic Principles of Justice for Victims of Crime and Abuse of Power and called for every effort to implement it.

It is possible that if the police and the justice system were reshaped to improve the assistance to victims, there could be an increase in the reporting of crimes and therefore in police knowledge of crimes. Ultimately, these principles of justice call for much better ways of meeting the needs of victims following a crime than tough-on-crime policies, as we will see in greater detail in Chapter 6.

Cumulatively, the harm to victims and the costs to the public are immense. The harm to victims seems impossible to quantify emotionally, but economists have developed ways to put a financial cost on these human experiences by estimating what a civil court would have ordered in tort action. In the United States, the costs of common crime were estimated at $425 billion per year in 1994. This was an average of $4,000 per family. Today several countries provide estimates of these costs that take into account the "anticipatory measures," such as having to procure private security (about 10%), the "consequences," such as the impact on victims of loss and suffering and community decay (about 70%), and "responses," such as operating expenditures on policing, courts, and corrections (about 20%).

It is also possible to estimate the cumulative costs of particular types of offenses. Because the rate of homicide in the United States per 100,000 is so high (nearly three times that of other Western democracies), it is a major contributor to the costs of overall crime within its borders. In all countries, sexual offenses contribute significantly, though the order of magnitude is increased significantly when one uses crime victimization survey data, which we discussed earlier in this chapter, rather than police data as so many victims do not report sexual offenses to the police.

TOUGH ON TAXPAYERS

According to statistics by the BJS shown in Figure 1.3, the expenditures on responses that use law and order have grown inexorably over the past twenty years.[1] At election time, your politician was increasing your tax burden when he promised to be tougher on crime by hiring more police officers, enacting minimum sentences, or keeping repeat offenders behind bars. Figure 1.3 shows just how tough it has become to you as taxpayers. Even if you adjust the figures for inflation by using what the economists call "constant dollars," the direct expenditures on police have more than doubled, while the expenditures on incarceration have more than tripled.

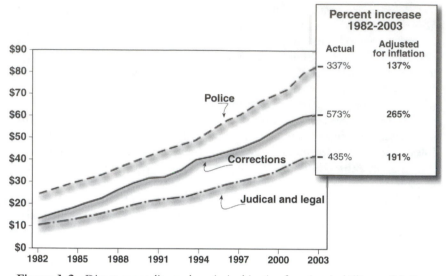

Figure 1.3. Direct expenditures by criminal justice function in billions of dollars, 1982–2003.

The average U.S. taxpayer today pays twice what the average British or Canadian taxpayer pays, even though thirty years ago the amounts were similar. The striking irony is that it is the U.S. taxpayers who have the reputation of being the most committed to cutting back on government. Why would less government equate more law and order? It does not make sense.

Here is what U.S. taxpayers are paying more for. They are paying $83 billion a year for 708,000 full-time sworn law enforcement officers at the state and local levels.[2] From 1980 to 2000, the numbers had grown by a staggering 54 percent—much more than any increase in population or crime could justify. The increase of 230,000 more officers at an average cost of $90,000 per officer is equivalent to more than $25 billion in taxes. In the same time period, police numbers in Canada grew by only 6 percent and in England and Wales by only 12 percent. These statistics date from 2003 but many more officers have been hired in the government's efforts to respond to the threat of terrorism following 9/11.

The taxes allocated to judicial and legal services now exceed $41 billion per year. The increase alone is almost $24 billion. In this case, the workload increase was a relatively modest 9 percent in adult courts, where most of the funds are expended. It seems the lawyers looked after themselves better than police or incarceration.

But the increases in tax dollars allocated to law enforcement and lawyers pale in comparison to the escalation in the use of incarceration that took place in the United States. This can only be described as "hyperincarceration" as it exaggerates the use of this scarce resource to such a degree that the United States became the world's number one jailer. In those two decades from 1980 to 2000, the number of adults incarcerated in the United States in federal, state, and local institutions rose by an amazing 290 percent to more than 2 million. The increase in numbers just from 1980 to 2000 is one and a half million more than the total population of Philadelphia and exceeds the population of thirteen states.

Comparisons between the United States and other countries show how much has changed.[3] If we divide those 2 million by the current population of the United States, it works out to a rate of over 700 per 100,000 inhabitants. The rate is now higher than that for Russia or China, usually thought of as the most oppressive societies, five times that of England and Wales and seven times that of Canada or the European Union. The quadrupling in the United States makes the 33 percent increase in Canada and 53 percent increase in England and Wales look meager.

Not surprisingly, the annual bill to taxpayers for incarceration has reached an astronomical $61 billion per year in 2003. Based on the average expenditures, the increase in taxes spent is equivalent to $43 billion each year—one and a half million at $28,500 per inmate per year. This is to say nothing of the costs of prison construction: Additional cells had to be built at a cost of between $50,000 and $100,000 each. Even if only half a million additional cells were built, the construction costs would range between $25 and $50 billion.

The grand total for police, courts, and corrections in the United States was at $186 billion in 2003—the latest year for which expenditures are publicly available—and so must be over $200 billion by now just with a 5 percent annual increase. The increase from 1982 to 2003 was already 165 percent after discounting for inflation—that is, the average U.S. taxpayer is paying more than two and a half times what they paid twenty years ago. By 2003, the cost alone of the additional police officers, inmates, and lawyers relative to 1982 was $91 billion each year—$25 billion for extra police, $24 billion for judicial and legal expenditures, and $42 billion for increased numbers of inmates incarcerated. By 2006, I estimate—BJS has not yet published official figures—that U.S. taxpayers are paying in excess of $100 billion for the increases in sworn police officers and inmates incarcerated and associated extra legal costs that have occurred since 1980.[4]

While most of the taxes are collected and most of the expenditures occur at the state and local levels, these huge increases were driven by Federal policies that themselves doubled to encourage the other levels of government to spend more. For instance, the Clinton administration increased nationally the number of law enforcement officers by 20 percent or 100,000 officers by providing the initial funds to state and local governments who, as will be shown in Chapter 5, were duped to take them on.

According to the BJS, 8 percent of state and local taxes go for police, courts, and corrections, that is, slightly more than taxes on health and hospitals. Yes, much less than the 30 percent of taxes that went for education and 14 percent for public welfare. But, I particularly like the comparison with health and hospitals, because it is a statement that politicians act as if police, courts, and corrections are more important than our health. Also the spending of taxes on police, courts, and corrections is not subject to the same controls as expenditures on health care, which must respect many controls from government on the effectiveness of the treatments given. The doctors, nurses, and so on have to qualify on exams that require them to know what works to reduce disease and not just respond to disease. Further, some significant rationalization—cuts in expenditures of taxes—has occurred in the health area as governments realized that they could not afford to expand the number of beds in hospitals forever. In the crime area, governments have expanded the number of cells for incarceration forever, almost without any checks and certainly without considering the truth and good sense about the alternatives.

But this is not the end of the costs to taxpayers, some of whom are paying for private security as individuals or through corporations. There are more than 2 million employees in the private security industry in the United States—likely costing them another $100 billion. They are also paying for alarms and other security gadgets and insurance against theft and other crimes. Unfortunately, there are no reliable estimates of these totals. Relative to population, these are not so different from Canada or England and Wales.

Many Americans purchase handguns for protection, unlike the British or the Canadians. So Americans pay more taxes for police, prisoners, and judges, then pay for private security, and then arm themselves. Does this make any sense if the knowledge exists to reduce victimization significantly?

TOUGH TO GET RESULTS

Despite this growth in tax expenditures, it is difficult to get results through the standard system of police, prisons, and judges for a variety of reasons that have been demonstrated in several presidential commissions and reports from the Surgeon General and the National Research Council.

Following the assassinations of President John Kennedy, Senator Robert Kennedy, and civil rights activist Martin Luther King Jr. in the 1970s, the United States set up major inquiries into who was responsible, which have become well known to the reading public as they leaf through pages of real-life detective stories. Less well known to the public but easily accessible to politicians are the pathbreaking presidential commissions that were developed to identify recommendations for action based on knowledge, and best thinking about the causes and solutions to violence. These commissions produced very similar recommendations that are important in understanding why more police, prisons, and judges make little difference to the rates of crime and victimization.

The commissions were about crime, the offenders, and victims and what could be done about them.[5] Their conclusions were as much about improving law enforcement and criminal justice as about tackling the risk factors that cause crime before citizens are victimized. They saw crime and violence as the result of risk factors exacerbated by poverty, discrimination, unsatisfactory schooling and housing, as well as an ill-equipped and disorganized law enforcement system. They made recommendations about how these "causes" of crime and violence could be addressed, what the police, courts, and corrections industry needed to do, and ways to modernize the tackling of crime.

The main effort to implement the recommendations came in 1968, when the U.S. Congress passed its major and comprehensive act to establish the Law Enforcement Assistance Administration (LEAA). This primarily provided federal funds to assist state and local actions to pay more for law enforcement—law and order—and did little to tackle either the root causes or risk factors. The salaries of police officers and correctional personnel have been raised from below the average household income in the United States to above the average household income. The working conditions of police, lawyers, and correctional professionals have significantly improved through training, job-related innovation, and multiple new buildings.

Their call for a more scientific approach has been heeded in part with investments in computer technology in police cars, in managing caseloads in courts, and in locks, surveillance cameras, and electronic monitoring for prisoners and offenders. A small proportion of the funds has even gone into research on the effectiveness of police, courts, and corrections. They did put funds into better data so that we have data from the BJS that have been used in this chapter on rates of crime, proportion of victimizations reported to police, and expenditures on police, courts, and corrections.

Unfortunately, however, their call for efforts to tackle the risk factors that cause crime was largely ignored. True, many general social policies were introduced for other reasons than preventing crime to tackle poverty, discrimination, and so on. But these miss the central point that it is not poverty that causes crime, though it does put some youth more at risk to committing offenses.

These commissions, and the development of criminology as a discipline, have sparked some useful—though little used—research into crime, generally in the years that followed. The problem is that the knowledge has only stimulated a patchwork of pilot projects, many of which disappear after the project has demonstrated success and the initial funding runs out. Criminology as a discipline has focused more on scientific studies than on ways to put their knowledge into action. However, it has led to a growing body of research on the effectiveness of policing in the United States, the United Kingdom, and

Australia and ultimately the report by the National Research Council on the *Fairness and Effectiveness in Policing* in 2004, which will help us establish the truth in Chapter 5.[6] Generally its conclusions are that the "standard" model of policing does not impact on crime. The standard model is one where the police use their resources—65 percent locally—to respond to calls made to an emergency number—911—and secondarily for detectives. The standard model does not include any significant funding for police to try to resolve crime problems by tackling risk factors that cause crime. The best police chiefs in England and Wales are used to advise the government on ways to improve policing. In 1998, they examined whether police were *Beating Crime*[7] and came to the same conclusion as the researchers in the United States that it was rare for the police to make a difference to the levels of crime.

Their conclusions epitomize a number of realities of policing that make it difficult for the standard model to succeed in preventing crime:

- Many victims of crime do not call the police and so the police are not aware of many crimes.
- Police officers rarely detect "street" crimes—one estimate shows a police officer to be within 100 yards of a burglary only once every eight years.
- Police officers are unlikely to be present to deter wife battering and child abuse because these occur behind closed doors where police are not present.
- Police investigators are so inundated with files that they rely on convicting culprits who are known rather than detective work to find those who are not known.

But what about correcting the behavior of the offenders who are convicted? In the corrections area, research has been conducted on a much larger scale over a longer period of time. Already by the mid-1970s, scientific research had accumulated in England and California looking at the effectiveness of standard prison programs, community sanctions such as probation and parole, and innovative intervention strategies. The British Home Office had completed scientific evaluations of Borstals—a three-year prison experience for young adults—and detention centers—a three-month boot camp—by the 1960s. My own research in Canada funded by the Ford Foundation evaluated whether incarceration reduced recidivism after release.

These evaluations showed that more than half of the graduates from standard corrections programs would be rearrested within three years of release. They also showed that the offenders who were reconvicted tended to be younger, with a longer offending history and with few community attachments. They not only concluded that incarceration did not reduce recidivism—reoffending—but also that after release, outcomes were largely determined by the life experiences of the men before they were arrested.[8] The implications of this conclusion have been overlooked. It points out that if you want to prevent crime, it is better to tackle the reasons why persons offend than to wait till they offend and then try to correct them.

More than anything, these large-scale and sophisticated evaluations showed that programs like prison or boot camps do not work. Interestingly, they showed that community sanctions such as fines worked better. Like in policing research, they showed that well-targeted programs which tackled established risk factors reduced the likelihood of a convicted offender returning to a life of crime.

Today the vast majority of resources in corrections still go into standard incarceration programs whose impact on crime is nothing more than keeping offenders off the street. Those U.S. states with the highest levels of incarceration are the ones with the highest levels of property and violent crimes, and not the reverse. For instance, Texas and Louisiana have the highest incarceration rates in the United States and are in the top six for rates of murder. Yes, the more persons incarcerated, the higher the property and violent crime rates. So, generally, more crime causes more incarceration rather than the reverse.

Nevertheless, incarceration provides an important, even if small, protection from crime because offenders behind bars cannot commit offenses in the community. I agree with the sophisticated analysis of the impact of incarceration rates on the drop in violent crime in the United States prepared by Spelman for the National Consortium on Violence Research. This demonstrates that the threefold—290 percent—increase in the number of persons incarcerated on an average day may have reduced crime rates by 27 percent in total.[9] Yet, the $43 billion increase to taxpayers of the hyperincarceration policy is gargantuan—enough, according to the National Consortium on Violence Research Group, to provide a job to every unemployed youth or childcare for the poor. In the following chapters, I will show that the prestigious commissions provide proof and good sense as to how these funds could be spent along similar lines but focus better to tackle proven research factors to achieve even larger reductions in crime and victimization.

But there is another factor that makes it difficult and expensive for the police, prisons, and judges to prevent crime. There is an unavoidable and dramatic attrition in cases from initial victimization to a conviction in a court. Even the BJS has not brought this information together. So it will be illustrated with a figure taken from a widely distributed report by the British Home Office (see Figure 1.4).[10]

In England an average of 45 percent of victimizations are reported to the police—a proportion similar to that of the United States. Studies have shown that not all victimizations reported to the police get recorded, and so they estimate that only 24 percent of the original victimizations will be recorded. The clearance rate in England is as low as in the United States, and so only 20 percent of these offenses result in the police knowing who the perpetrator

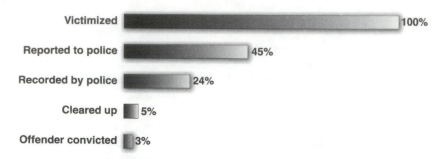

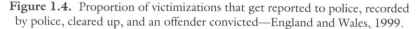

Figure 1.4. Proportion of victimizations that get reported to police, recorded by police, cleared up, and an offender convicted—England and Wales, 1999.

was. Of these, they estimate about 50 percent will result in a conviction in a court. So the end result is that only 3 percent of victimizations will result in a conviction. This data overlooks the fact that persistent offenders who commit many offenses in a year will have a much higher risk of getting convicted than that of 3 percent. Some research suggests that this may get as high as 50 percent for property offenses. When police target suspects who have many previous convictions, they increase their chances of catching the persistent offenders. But the end result is that you need to investigate huge numbers of victimizations to stand a chance of incarcerating a few offenders.

But the 27 percent decrease in crime and victimization demonstrated by the Violence Research Group was not just achieved by increased expenditures of $43 billion on prisoners but also required large increases in law enforcement and judicial activities. In sum, the 27 percent decrease in crime came from the $100 billion increase in taxes that I identified in the previous section. You need more police officers to catch more of the known offenders and more judges and lawyers to determine whether they are guilty or not.

"TOUGH ON CAUSES" IS TOUGHER ON CRIME

What else could we have done with $100 billion that would have achieved a larger reduction in victimization for everyone, with more positive benefits for young disadvantaged males? Would it be better to invest in helping youth at risk, empowering women and children to avoid violence, supporting community groups to stop crime, training police to use problem-oriented tactics, or ensuring that victims have rights?

The frustrating thing is that scientists and even prestigious commissions agree that we have the knowledge on how to use that $100 billion to reduce crime to the rates of the early 1960s. We do not need to suffer the trauma and loss as victims if we put this knowledge to work. Unfortunately, criminologists have been too concerned with science and not enough with getting knowledge applied. The political elite have continued to do more of the same regardless of its ineffectiveness. However, some pioneers have put this knowledge to work. The later chapters of this book will show how some jurisdictions are already doing this, and how this could become a reality for all of us without any increase in taxes.

What is the basis for knowing how to reinvest those funds to reduce crime? Following the economic expansion of the 1970s and the associated growth in government, in the 1980s policymakers began to be concerned about the extent to which their spending was delivering results. Various types of governmental spending reviews began to question their core expenditures. The most impressive of these in relation to crime and justice is undoubtedly the British Audit Commission with its report on *Misspent Youth* in 1996, which made use of an accumulation of knowledge, particularly from the United States and also a growing realization by mayors in Europe and the United States, that crime could not be solved just by more police, prisons, and judges but required an investment in tackling the risk factors that cause crime before people were victimized.

Gilbert Bonnemaison, a national politician and mayor from France, was the lightning rod mobilizing mayors on both sides of the Atlantic to realize that this broader and more balanced approach was needed and would succeed. He led with my help two international conferences in Montreal in 1989 and in Paris in 1991 that radically transformed the way in which some governments were to look at crime and its solution. The momentum for the conferences came from mayors of big cities in Europe, Canada, and the United States, who had become alarmed by the rapid and continued growth in crime. They felt that limiting the solutions to law and order was a major reason for the lack of solutions. They also felt that centralized law-and-order solutions missed what could be done locally. They wanted to bring together different agencies working in schools, housing, and so on.

Before each conference, material was brought together on various projects that had already been shown to have worked—and not worked—such as a preschool program called the Perry Preschool in Michigan and the national job creation program called Job Corps.[11] For instance, for the Paris conference, I wrote the opening address on putting crime prevention on the map and to work while Philippe Robert—the top French criminologist at the time—orchestrated an international scientific review of prevention and what had worked to reduce crime.[12]

These conferences articulated a "tough on causes, tough on crime" vision and mobilized considerable knowledge about what works in tackling risk factors. I worked with Gilbert Bonnemaison and others to launch a permanent international center that would bring together best practice and articulate the strong arguments to invest in prevention. Just three years after the Paris conference, the French and Canadian governments were persuaded to launch the innovative International Centre for the Prevention of Crime (ICPC), of which I became the founding chief executive and Gilbert Bonnemaison the chair of its board. Today, the ICPC is affiliated with the United Nations and is supported by a consortium of Western European, North American, Latin American, and African governments.

The ICPC was built around a considerable knowledge of what had worked and of how to put it into practice. It was the materials from these conferences that formed the core of the library and legitimacy of the ICPC which was asked to share its information and vision with several different commissions. It brought together inspiring examples of successes from both sides of the Atlantic in several different languages and developed the arguments as to why governments should invest in prevention. It emphasized the research that had showed that prevention in the community that tackles risk factors is much more cost-effective than standard policing and prisons.

The ICPC's conclusions were clear that significant increases or decreases in the levels of the standard police, courts, and corrections programs do not have any significant impact on crime, but that many prevention projects investing in youth at risk and designing out crime had reduced crime. Further, the evaluations of these projects often showed that they were more cost-effective than standard policing, courts, and corrections. Importantly, they also showed that the solutions to crime lay in getting community agencies such as schools, housing, social services, and police to identify the risk factors that cause crime and collaboratively work on solutions. The ICPC's material was available in unpublished and published reports that eventually became *100 Crime Prevention Programs from Across the World* and the *Digest II: Comparative Analysis of Successful Community Safety*.[13]

The ICPC and its network used this knowledge to influence several other commissions who would double-check the conclusions. The first and strategically important commission to verify the facts and the vision was England's independent Audit Commission, which examined whether taxes for local government were being used in the best way to produce results in its study of the operation of standard police, courts, and corrections, in relation to young offenders. Because of the ICPC's material and its contacts, the Audit Commission was able to look at a significant amount of research accumulated on both sides of the Atlantic. Its conclusions were published in the seminal report titled *Misspent Youth* in 1996.[14] This poignant title reflects the conclusion that the spending was too much too late. The evidence shows that the spending that works is focused on youth at risk of offending, before they offend.

Just a few years later, the ICPC influenced a joint working group between the British Home Office and Treasury in 1997, when it was deciding where and how to invest funds for reducing crime in England.[15] The Home Office had a large team of experienced researchers who were assigned the task of reviewing all the research in various areas such as childcare, teenagers, housing design, policing, and corrections. These careful reviews were subjected to a special test at a workshop attended by international experts and key players from the prime minister's office and Treasury. Their conclusions were the same as that of the Audit Commission in many ways, though their insistence on having research results to use meant that they downplayed the role of interagency approaches to crime prevention, which are not easy to assess using classic research methods. They also brought together research on how crime can be designed out through CCTV (closed-circuit television), car alarms, and so on.

In 1996, Professor Del Elliott launched a program called "Blue Prints" for violence prevention.[16] The Center for the Study and Prevention of Violence got funding from the Centers for Disease Control (CDC) and the Colorado Division of Criminal Justice (and later from the Pennsylvania Commission on Crime and Delinquency). It is no accident that so many of the successful initiatives to put knowledge to work came from sources that were not criminology, which has contributed knowledge but too often not to action.

The Blue Prints is only one of the initiatives of CDC to introduce a public health perspective into efforts to prevent injury. Overall, Blue Prints' work focuses on injuries and fatalities from violence but with a perspective of what is the best way to reduce these injuries and fatalities rather than how much punishment should be meted out in what form. Today, its Web site brings information on epidemiology and prevention to bear on child maltreatment, intimate partner violence, sexual violence, and youth violence. Although it makes reference to law enforcement strategies, most of the material highlighted by this initiative deals with the role of public health nurses and education as well as the need for a holistic analysis of the problem.

The aim of Blue Prints was to identify ten violence prevention programs that met a very high scientific standard of program effectiveness—programs that could provide an initial nucleus for a national violence prevention initiative. Its objective was to identify truly outstanding programs, and to describe these interventions in a series of "blueprints." On its Web site, you can find practical descriptions of the selected programs that set out the theoretical rationale, the core components of the program as implemented, the evaluation designs and results, and the practical experiences programs encountered while implementing the program at multiple sites. Blue Prints allows states, communities, and individual agencies to determine if the program is appropriate for them, in addition to the organizational capacity and funding needed. It also includes some indication of potential difficulties that may limit the success of the program. The Office of Juvenile Justice and Delinquency Prevention of the U.S. Department of Justice wanted to fund replications of Blue Prints project in other jurisdictions.

These reports were also joined by a report prepared by a consortium of criminology professors. The U.S. Department of Justice was required to provide the U.S. Congress with an independent review of its financial assistance programs to state and local crime prevention—which meant as much law and order as it did precrime prevention. This was organized by the National Institute of Justice (NIJ)—the remnant of the research arm of the old LEAA program. NIJ contracted with Larry Sherman, an energetic research criminologist, and his colleagues at the University of Maryland to undertake the analysis.[17] Sherman is a strong believer in experimental research where scientists use randomized controlled trials (RCTs) to test whether a law enforcement or preventive intervention works. An RCT is a field experiment where the subjects of an innovative intervention, such as a program to avoid youth at risk of dropping out of school, are selected at random from a pool of eligible youth so that the scientists can determine whether the intervention was the only experience responsible for a change in an outcome such as offending. It is similar to the techniques used by health departments to test whether a drug works. Sherman is also a convincing orator who later rose to be president of both the American Society of Criminology and the International Society of Criminology. The conclusions from Sherman and his colleagues are particularly important because they reaffirm that the vast majority of the "standard" police, courts, and corrections programs do not work or at least do not have any evidence to show that they are able to reduce crime. However, where scientific comparisons are made between innovations tackling risk factors thought to cause crime and the standard programs, the innovations are proven to lower crime rates. Where there were evaluations of the standard programs, they did not produce significant reductions in crime.

To assess the scientific research, Sherman and his colleagues developed a five-point scale for assessing the reliability of the evidence from particular evaluations. According to them, the conclusions of the effectiveness of a program are stronger; the larger the number of persons (such as youth at risk) that went through the program, the more often the programs have been tested in different locations, and the more the results were evaluated by an independent expert who compared the results for those who went through the program with a similar or identical group of persons. The conclusions from Sherman and his colleagues echo the conclusions from reviews twenty years earlier that had already shown that standard corrections did not work, but that programs targeted to risk factors that cause crime might work if given sufficient resources.[18]

Their reports like the ICPC material and *Misspent Youth* that went before them were positive on what was working. Its original title, "What Works, What Does Not and What Is Promising," reflects the reality that many innovative programs such as those that tackle risk factors such as dropping out of school for youth do in fact work. However, Sherman inimitably called for a greater investment in research and development, using RCTs rather than greater investment in what does work and what makes sense. What a pity for victims and taxpayers!

This knowledge from *Misspent Youth*, ICPC, Blue Prints, and Sherman becomes more powerful by its consolidation and adoption by a wider group of prestigious organizations, many of whom published reports around the year 2000. The following list shows the prestigious organizations that issued reports. We would have confidence in these organizations on other issues—so why not on crime. They include the

- U.S. Surgeon General on Youth Violence;
- U.S. National Association of Attorneys General on School Violence;
- U.S. Centers for Disease Control on Best Practices on Youth Violence Prevention;
- Institute of Public Policy for the State of Washington on the Comparative Costs and Benefits of Programs to Reduce Crime.

Also important are reports published by equally prestigious organizations in England and Wales, including Her Majesty's Inspectorate of Constabulary (HMIC), the Home Office, and other reports by the Audit Commission. HMIC is particularly interesting as it is made up of the most distinguished police chiefs in England, often including the commissioner of Scotland Yard. Yet they concluded, as we will see in more detail in Chapter 5, that standard policing had no evidence to support its efficacy while affirming that policing could impact significantly on crime if it focused more on risk factors that cause crime.

In 2002, the World Health Organization (WHO)—a body in which we have confidence—published its major report on Health and Violence to be followed by another report on implementation of the world report. In 2004, WHO published another report on traffic fatalities and injuries.[19] These reports use similar material and come to clear conclusions that violence is not an accident; it is preventable. Their recommendations stress the importance of better planning and data about crime and violence. In 2002, the U.N. Office on Drugs and Crime Prevention adopted guidelines for crime prevention that take these a step further by identifying what must be done at all levels of government to achieve real reductions in crime and victimization.

If these are not enough, the National Research Council (U.S.) issued several major reports, covering violence in families, juvenile crime, school violence, and effectiveness of policing. This council has existed since 1916. Its main role is to review all the research in an area—not just crime—and then make recommendations for policy, practice, and research. It selects a broad committee of twenty distinguished academics in the United States to be members of its oversight committee on issues such as law and justice, and then this group selects the specialized committees, such as the most recent one on policing to review research on police policy and practice.

All of these commissions arrive at specific and even actionable conclusions which we will now look into in the following chapters. There are many positive conclusions about precrime prevention programs, designing out crime, and use of police as problem solvers. There are recommendations about the role that cities can play in delivering more effective crime prevention at a lower cost to taxpayers. There are recommendations about how victims can be treated consistent with the principles of justice agreed to at the United Nations.

Unfortunately, governments continue to misspend our taxes on expensive and largely ineffective ways of reducing crime instead of on what will reduce crime in a sustainable manner. These reports provide an extensive body of knowledge about the risk factors that cause crime as well as interventions that have tackled those risk factors, and so prevent persons from becoming persistent offenders or being victims of crime. It is these bodies of knowledge that will help us know how taxes could be used more effectively to reduce victimization. They show, particularly, how programs targeted to high-risk areas have been able to reduce crime. Unfortunately, criminological researchers often miss the ways in which knowledge can be put into practice. This book is about how to use that knowledge to reduce victimization.

IN CONCLUSION

There was a rapid decline in violent victimization in the 1990s in the United States as in England and Wales and Canada. In the United States, the trends set off a wave of claims by Giuliani and others that they had achieved miracles. Even so, crime and victimization still affects one in four adults each year and remains a serious and costly problem for the victims.

In the United States, taxpayers now pay significantly more for law enforcement and incarceration than they had in 1980. The increase is paying for an additional number of police officers and an extra 1.5 million persons incarcerated. The additional cost alone exceeds $100 billion a year.

It is difficult for these expenditures to have a significant impact on victimization, as so many crimes are not reported to the police, and so few crimes recorded are cleared. Nevertheless, the 300 percent increase in incarceration may have produced a 27 percent decrease in crime rates.

An accumulation of prestigious commissions have looked at what are the risk factors that cause crime and the success that has been achieved through preventive interventions. It is these commissions that form the basis for the next six chapters that will discuss more effective ways of using this $100 billion that not only reduce victimization and provide better futures for youth, women, and children at risk, but also make further increases in taxes for law and order unnecessary.

2

Pay to Keep Kids from Crime, Not behind Bars

Judging by newspaper headlines, criminals are getting tougher and younger. It is not just boys, now it is also girls. They join vicious gangs that are at war with each other. They get access to handguns which they use to kill each other. They steal cars that are used in high-speed rodeos and fatal police chases. They bully until their victims rebel. They sexually assault.

The law and order advocates define these kids as evil. They point to the lack of discipline at home and the emasculation of teachers who are no longer able to impose discipline because they do not have access to corporal punishment. They call for tougher penalties from the courts and more short, sharp, shock punishments. Indeed, in the United States and in a few cases elsewhere, they have gotten their way. State governments have invested in military-style boot camps where wayward youth will be disciplined. Ten thousand youth in the United States will be sent to an adult court for trial and punishment because their offense was so serious. Another 90,000 or more will be incarcerated on an average day.

As early as 1961, the Broadway musical *West Side Story* romanticized the violence between rival gangs in the Bronx. While the weapons were knives rather than handguns and the gangs were based on Latino rather than black identities, the insights were surprisingly correct. The words in the conversation with the local police sergeant in "Gee, Officer Krupke" epitomize the debate about youth offending. The song debates whether the kid's delinquency comes from him or her being evil, unwanted by his or her parents, brought up by drunk and dissolute parents, or just growing through a difficult age. It debates solutions that include social work, psychiatry, or a job. Yes, it includes a year in prison.

While the song ends in frustration by rejecting all those solutions, the research since 1961 has enabled the prestigious commissions to come to strong conclusions about what are the early and late development experiences predispose a child to persistent offending. They also agree on which evaluations of projects have successfully tackled the results of these development experiences to prevent crime. So in this chapter we will first look at what puts kids at risk of committing offenses and then what projects have been able to tackle those risk factors.

FAMILY AND SCHOOL EXPERIENCES THAT INFLUENCE RISK OF OFFENDING

In the last thirty years, we have been able to consolidate a significant amount of scientific knowledge about which experiences at home and school influence the likelihood of a young person getting involved in offending.[1] There are several of these experiences, risk factors, or causes. There is no single cause. The predictions of later delinquency based on these risk factors are about as accurate as predictions of epidemiologists forecasting who will get lung cancer based on weight, income, or smoking habits.[2] This confidence in knowing what causes people to offend comes from impressive large-scale surveys painstakingly done by scientists in England, the United States, and elsewhere. The surveys have become known as "longitudinal" because they research the development of thousands of children longitudinally from birth to adolescence. The surveys are undertaken by scientists both in government agencies as well as in university centers.

Professionals completing and analyzing these longitudinal surveys talk to tens of thousands of children and youth in the same systematic manner—collecting the same data and asking the same questions. They record the various developmental experiences of the children through all stages of their childhood, primary and secondary school, and later life. With permission, data are also obtained from doctors and hospitals from which the children received medical care. Data are collected from their schools about their performance, peers, and discipline, and from their parents about upbringing and attitudes. In adolescence, checks are made with the police to collect data on whether they have been arrested or charged with an offense. Some scientists also follow adult achievements and difficulties. The data are then used to see statistically what experiences preceded their involvement in crime, particularly if it was persistent.

One of the most recent and largest of these surveys was underway in Chicago in the 1990s under the direction of Felton Earls, a professor in the School of Public Health at Harvard University. Titled the Project on Human Development in Chicago Neighborhoods, it followed 7,000 children and youth over an eight-year period. The study did not only look at the developmental pathways that predispose some children to become involved in persistent delinquency but also at how community ties and relationships affect these pathways. It had a particular focus on how exposure to violence affects the outcomes.

The most robust source of knowledge for policymaking comes from analyzing the conclusions from several of these "longitudinal" studies. This technique has the sophisticated name of meta-analysis. When the scientist looks at several studies, the confidence in the conclusions grows. Instead of it being based on one study of 25,000, it is based on several studies with several hundreds of thousands of subjects. As the nature of the experiences that are shown to predispose the persons to crime is similar between the studies, the conclusions provide a robust source of knowledge on what needs to be tackled to reduce crime.

The most important finding from the longitudinal surveys is that a small group of children born each year will account for a disproportionate number of the offenses—5–10 percent of children accounting for 50–70 percent of all the offenses admitted by the children or known to the police as the children grow up and become young adults. This 5–10 percent subgroup is often referred to as persistent offenders as their behavior gets them in conflict with the police frequently.[3]

The children who become persistent offenders tend to grow up with more negative family and school experiences, such as being

- born into a family in relative poverty and inadequate housing;
- brought up with inconsistent and uncaring parenting, including violence;
- with limited social and cognitive abilities;
- with behavioral problems identified in primary school;
- excluded from, or dropping out of, secondary school;
- living with a culture of violence on television and in the neighborhood;
- frequently unemployed and with relatively limited income as a young adult.

This is not to excuse the behavior, as many with these disadvantages choose not to commit offenses and others without these disadvantages do. However, these studies do not show law and order interventions such as arrest or incarceration reducing offending in a cost-effective manner. In fact, the more times a person is arrested, the more likely they are to be arrested in the future. So, law enforcement is not a significant way to deter their offending, though it is a significant way to identify who is offending after they have repeat-offended. Yes, hyperincarceration of these offenders will reduce offending while they are incarcerated but it follows the multiple victimizations that are needed for law enforcement to catch them. A better way is to tackle the proven risk factors and so help more kids to flourish. This will prevent the multiple victimizations.

INVEST IN PARENTING AND CHILD DEVELOPMENT

In the United States alone, at least 900,000 children will be victims of mal-treatment, often perpetrated by their parents or caregivers. This staggering number in the world's richest and most powerful country calls for greater attention. In addition, we know that children who are victims or even witnesses of violence at home are more likely up than other adults to be violent when they grow.[4]

In the 1980s, I used the example of the Perry Preschool Program because it developed a scientific experiment—randomized control trial (RCT)—to show that children who went through the program when they were 3 and 4 years old were much more likely to stay crime free when they were adolescents. The program itself consisted of enriched child care that would help the children develop without the disadvantages of inconsistent and uncaring parenting. The child care was provided by qualified child-care workers—many with university degrees—who focused on a maximum of eight children for at least two and half hours a day. It provided self-initiated learning activities that encourage sound intellectual and social development.

The RCT started with 123 low-income African American children who were at high risk of school failure. Half of the children were randomly assigned to the program and half were left as a control group. The scientific evaluator then compared what happened to the children who experienced the preschool program with the comparison group in their adolescent years and indeed now up to age 40.[5]

This powerful scientific method demonstrated that only 36 percent of those going through the program had five or more arrests by age 40 compared to 55 percent for the comparison group. That is, the program at age 3 and 4 caused a 34 percent reduction in arrests by age 40. This amazing result suggests that a policy would significantly reduce crime and victimization if it multiplied the number of these preschool programs in neighborhoods that have many children at risk in terms of the factors identified in the longitudinal surveys. The crime prevention effect was equally powerful in adolescence and early adulthood up to age 27. This reduction in arrests nationally saved $15 in the costs of police, prisons, and judges for every dollar originally invested. An ounce of prevention is proved here to equal almost a pound (15 instead of 16 oz) in savings of reaction—also amazing.

For statisticians, this scientific trial is more than enough to prove that enriched child care prevents crime. The difference in arrest rates between those who went through the program and those who did not only occurred less than one in a thousand times. However, when I debated these results with a public servant who had to advise Prime Minister Blair on a policy, he was not convinced that a sample of fifty-eight children from a suburb of Detroit, which has a murder rate twenty times that of London, was enough on which to base a national policy.

I agree with the caution, but the real implication of Perry Preschool is not the remedy but the illustration that when one tackles a well-established risk factor, one can reduce crime. The studies demonstrating the importance of the risk factor are based on samples of tens of thousands. So my conclusion is: Identify the risk factor and then work on the remedy but be inspired by the amazing results from Perry Preschool.

In briefing the political elite, I prefer to use the example of the Chicago Child–Parent Center Program that did not use a scientific trial (RCT) but did involve much larger numbers of children. It is also an example of a successful project to reduce the impact of inconsistent and uncaring parenting for younger children. The superintendent of the Chicago Public School board founded the Child–Parent Center Program in 1967 to help disadvantaged children get ready for elementary school. It is one of the oldest federally funded preschool programs in the United States. It is an early intervention project that provides comprehensive educational and family-support services to economically disadvantaged children from preschool to early elementary school. The program is designed to serve families in high-poverty neighborhoods that are not being served by other early childhood programs. The overall goal of the program is to promote children's academic success and to facilitate parent involvement in children's education.

The Child–Parent Center Program had three components. First, trained professionals went out to meet disadvantaged families by going to their homes and organizing meetings where parents could come to learn about the program. This "outreach" strategy reaches the families that would not normally use the services. Second, they provided an enriched kindergarten experience for children with small class sizes and a focus on helping the child acquire language skills. The children participated for two and a half hours every day. Third, they insisted that the parents come to the center to learn how they could parent better.

Professor Arthur Reynolds and his colleagues scientifically compared the children invited into the project from the worst poverty areas of Chicago with a similar group of 550 children who went to an alternative kindergarten program. His funding came from the U.S. Department of Education and the University of Wisconsin. Seventeen percent of those who attended the program had been arrested by age 20 compared to 25 percent of the comparison group. So the Child–Parent Center Program may have contributed to a 32 percent reduction in arrests ([25–17]/25). The children who went to the center also completed school at a much higher rate and more often got jobs later on.

They also calculated the average cost of the program per child as $6,730 each year and demonstrated that the benefits were equal to $47,759. That is, a benefit of $7 over the lifetime of the participant for every dollar invested—a stitch in time saves seven in this case not nine. Half of these benefits are increases in lifetime earnings of $20,000, including $7,000 in taxes. Other savings identified included $7,000 for the justice system, $6,000 for crime victims, and $4,000 for special education.

The study included 989 children. So the cumulative savings equal $47 million, which is impressive enough. But for the total of 100,000 children who have passed through the Chicago Child–Parent Center Program since it started, this represents an impressive $4.7 billion in benefits. Just the increases in taxes paid by all these persons in their lifetime equals $700 million—ironically just short of being able to pay the budget of the Chicago Police Department of $1 billion for one year.

The strategy to prevent child abuse, which is best established in terms of scientific evidence, is sending a public health nurse or equivalent professional to visit the homes of high-risk families, particularly first-time parents. In 1977, Dr. Olds, a professor of pediatrics, psychiatry, and preventive medicine at the University of Colorado in Denver, led an impressive scientific study that demonstrated how public health nurses were more effective in reducing crime than were more police or prisons. He launched the study in Elmira, New York, a rural community of about 30,000 inhabitants. His subjects were 400 young women who were pregnant for the first time. They were teenagers or unmarried or from low-income families. He did his due diligence by analyzing the literature on what caused bad outcomes for the children; it was decided to use public health nurses who would visit the women to help with parenting practices, mental health problems, and use of tobacco and alcohol.

The study was not just an action project to help these women and their children, it was also an RCT study. So only 200 of the women received visits from the public health nurses. The other 200 were left to cope with help from the standard services in the community and so would be a comparison group. The analysis of the outcomes was continued for fifteen years after the experiment was started by comparing whether the children were abused and whether they were arrested in their teenage years.

During the time of the experiment, the nurses visited the women once every two weeks. Their task was to help the women understand fetal and child development as well as involve family and friends in providing support to the mother. There were an impressive 79 percent fewer reports of child abuse or neglect in the families of the children where the visits occurred than for the comparison group families. The results in preventing youth offending fifteen years later were equally impressive. The children of the mothers who received the visits had 56 percent fewer arrests than the control group by the age of 15.

The program was replicated in an African American community in Memphis, Tennessee, and a Mexican American community in Denver, Colorado. These replications also confirmed positive preventive effects of public health nurse visits. It is the state of Hawaii that is known for taking these data to heart and acting on them. Their "Healthy Start" program focused on a much larger group of 1,353 families who received a similar series of visitations by public health nurses with an associated 62 percent lower rate of child abuse and neglect.

The original program by Olds was estimated to cost $7,733 per family with net benefits of $15,916, without counting the savings to victims who were not abused as children. The cost of their program per family in Hawaii for the first two and a half years was less because there were economies in scale—only $3,200. To put this in perspective, the average annual cost of a police officer is $90,000. For equivalent of the salary of just one police officer, thirty families in at-risk areas could be receiving the benefit of the program. We will see in Chapter 5 that the National Research Council estimates that extra police officers cannot be justified at all in terms of crime reduction if they are used in standard policing strategies. However, when police officers are used to tackle risk factors that cause crime, they may reduce crime but not at anything close to the 62 percent level. Whatever the arithmetic, it is clear that all orders of government should be investing in this type of program, particularly for mothers who are at risk.

Olds is only one of several pioneers who have developed practical projects to assist kids who have lived through these negative experiences to get on with life successfully, where RCT has been used to confirm their effectiveness. Many of the prevention programs not only provide benefits in terms of crime reduction but also produce other socioeconomic benefits because the kids in the project go on more often to finish school and get jobs—to flourish. Unfortunately, the successful projects sometimes disappear after the success because politicians do not allocate new funds for them. Even if the project continues, it is rare for the politicians to build on the success by expanding the centers across their jurisdiction. It is a recurring theme of this book that these successes provide a rich arsenal for programs that politicians could use to achieve large reductions in crime with our taxes. Let's look more closely at overviews of these successes.

The scientific evidence on programs has been reviewed by many of the prestigious commissions. They often rely on the work of Professor Del Elliott at the University of Colorado at Boulder, whose team has specialized in reviewing the evidence from projects such as that of Olds and the Perry Preschool, so that they could identify successful projects that could become "Blue Prints" for the prevention of youth violence.[6] There are now eleven model programs that have met their rigorous selection criteria. In addition, a number of programs met only some of the criteria and were designated promising programs. The Blue Prints projects at the early childhood and at primary school level include the nurse visitation program developed by Olds because it had been replicated in another jurisdiction. Perry Preschool is only accepted as a promising program because it has not been replicated. The Chicago Child–Parent Center Program does not make the blueprint list as the evaluation did not use an RCT.

The Blue Prints project also includes using preschool and other programs to increase the cognitive and social abilities of children, particularly in underprivileged socioeconomic surroundings, and another one that increases support and respite for parents so that they are able to provide more consistent and caring discipline. Others focus on developing emotional skills for primary school children so that they can understand, express, and regulate their emotions. Although these have obtuse acronyms such as PATHS or Disney names such as Incredible Years, they are practical programs that enable very young children to cope better with anger and frustration.

Despite the strength of the science, the approval of prestigious commissions such as the National Research Council, and the ease of accessing the information, these cost-effective solutions to youth crime are not yet widely used. Instead the taxpayers' funds are still primarily used for the standard solutions that do not work as we saw in Chapter 1.

INVEST IN HELPING KIDS TO SUCCEED WITH MENTORS, SCHOOL, AND COLLEGE

The same is true for programs for teenagers. Much of the lives of children and adolescents are spent in school. Parents can do several things that will reduce the chances that their children will grow up committing many serious or even not so serious offenses. At the top of the list is that they can take an interest in their child, so that the children are more likely to complete school and weather difficulties with their peers, alcohol, and other substances. They can get assistance from the early years to provide consistent and caring parenting and take advantage of preschool programs as we have seen above. They can encourage the school administrations to doing everything to help children and teenagers complete school in safe surroundings as well as collaborate with their child and the school to tackle bullying.

The Blue Prints project has identified some important interventions at the teenage—secondary or high school—level which reduce offending. The most affordable one is to provide adult mentors to youth aged 6–18 who live in single-parent families below the poverty line. The blueprint status is based on the Big Brothers, Big Sisters program. The main activity consists of the mentor meeting with the youth for about four hours, three times a month and so providing a caring relationship and role model. The meeting is focused around activities that develop communication skills and relationships.

The evidence on the effectiveness of mentoring is based on a comparison between youth participating in the program with those on waiting lists. This showed that those mentored are 46 percent less likely to start using drugs and 32 percent less likely to hit someone. However, these are weak findings as they are not an RCT. The Institute for Public Policy (WSIPP)—a hybrid between a government audit office and research library for politicians in the state of Washington—undertook a review of over 400 evaluations of the cost-effectiveness of various prevention and treatment programs designed for youth at risk and juvenile offenders. They showed that for $1,054 spent for mentoring, they could identify net benefits of $4,524 in reduced costs to victims and the community. Thus mentoring is much more cost-effective than detention.

The most powerful evidence for mentoring that reduces offending comes from the poster boy RCT on testing the effectiveness of a program to help at-risk youth complete school. This included mentors as one of the key ingredients. Dr. Hahn, a professor in the School of Management and Social Policy at Brandeis University, was the evaluator of the program set up originally by Opportunities Industrialization Centers of America (OIC), often referred to as Quantum Opportunities. OIC itself was started in 1964 in an abandoned police station in Philadelphia. It has worked for forty years to help minority youth qualify to get into the job market. Hahn wanted to determine the extent to which an intensive program to prevent youth from dropping out of school would succeed and also reduce offending. The program started in 1989. It was done as a scientific experiment—an RCT—where twenty-five youth were selected at random for the program in each of Oklahoma City, Philadelphia, Saginaw, and San Antonio. The outcomes in terms of the proportion arrested were compared with a control group of the youth who were not selected.

The program started with youth in the ninth grade. It had three components for each of which 250 hours of activities were provided. First, academic skills were enhanced through tutoring and homework coaching. Second, life skills were developed, including assistance with life planning and job preparation. Third, volunteer activities were organized. Each participant had a caring adult mentor who stuck with him or her over the four years of the project. Financial incentives were used to encourage participation in the program at the rate of $1 an hour, but there were bonuses of $100 for completing some of the activities and a matching amount was put aside for activities after the program, such as training or college. Its primary purpose was to develop the life opportunities of the participants, where impressive results show many more participants completing school, receiving honors, and going onto post-secondary schools. The proportion of those arrested after completing the program was 70 percent below the proportion arrested in the control group. The cost of the program over four years was $10,600. This program was originally identified as a Blue Print Model Program but this is no longer the case. However, the program has been reviewed and analyzed by many of the prestigious commissions and so must remain as an important example to inspire action.

There are other programs that have so far only been given the promising program status by the Blue Prints project. For instance, "Families and Schools Together" is a program that has received many awards and has been recognized by the Office for Juvenile Justice and Delinquency Prevention of the U.S. Department of Justice as well as the U.S. Center for Substance Abuse as a promising program. It was developed to enhance family functioning by strengthening the parent–child relationship and empowering parents to become primary prevention agents for their children. It also prevents failure by the young persons at school by improving the young person's performance and empowering parents to support this process. It reduces the negative stress that families experience by developing an ongoing support group for parents and at-risk children.

In this model program, schools identify families that might benefit from the program. Professionals outreach to those families and invite them to join an eight- to fourteen-week process of activities designed from theory to achieve the goals. It uses parents who have already been through the program as well as those who are peers in the program as a key part of the process.

So the program costs per family are approximately $800—not only affordable but 100 families could be supported for the cost of one police officer—$80,000! Those involved in promoting the program believe that it will decrease violence, alcohol and other drug abuse, as well as child abuse and neglect. This seems probable. However, at this stage, no scientific evaluations are available to confirm this.

INVEST IN MAKING SCHOOLS SAFE FOR KIDS

Another Blue Print Model Program shows how to reduce bullying in schools. It is the only one of the Blue Prints to be modeled on a foreign success story. In this case, it is modeled on a national Norwegian program to reduce bullying. The irony of this model program is that it is well known across the world as a result of the Blue Prints program being promoted at the University of Colorado in Boulder. Yet it was not being used in Columbine High School, which is only an hour's drive away. It was at Columbine where one of the most horrible school shootings took place. This irony brings home more than anything how important it is to get action on the Blue Prints and other recommendations from the prestigious commissions.

On April 20, 1999, two bullied youth brought firearms into Columbine High School in the suburbs of Denver and massacred several of their fellow students. The Columbine massacre might not have happened if the school had been using the Blue Print on preventing bullying. More than any of the incidents in North America or Europe, the shootings at Columbine caught the imagination of the press. In fact, more than 99.9 percent of U.S. public schools have never had a homicide of any kind. Less than 1 percent of youth murders occur at school. Yet there is still a real bullying problem when up to 7 percent of eighth graders stay home from school at least once a month, out of fear of other students.

The Blue Print on preventing bullying is based on the success that the Norwegian government had in reducing violence in schools. In simple terms, the program was based on schoolteachers taking action to stop bullying.

They worked with both the bully and the victim to persuade them to stop. The first time there was a warning and discussion. The second time there was an attempt to find the cause with the parent and encourage family responsibility. The third time, the victim or bully was referred to a professional social worker. The result was a 50 percent reduction in bullying in Norway.

Following the Columbine incident, the National Association of Attorneys General (NAAG) of the United States listened to professionals on school safety and youth violence.[7] They heard how youth were more likely to be violent if they had witnessed domestic violence or had not received appropriate nurturing or had been bullied. As a national association of lawmakers and prosecutors, it is particularly remarkable to note how little they emphasized law and order and how much they emphasized actions by parents—even if they did not focus only on what has been proven to work. For instance, they called for parents to raise their children by listening, spending time, setting boundaries, and instilling values including respect for others. They wanted parents to network with other parents around issues of school discipline and improve their parenting skills. They wanted parents to pay attention to the movies, television, music, and Internet which their children watch or listen to, and to discuss the messages in these media. They wanted them to participate as mentors, coaches, and volunteers in the community to provide support for children. They wanted youth to influence peers and their juniors against violence, by being mentors, civil rights workers, and peer mediators to resolve disputes at their schools.

In desperation in the United States, the reaction of judges to youth who shoot their fellow students has been to sentence those youths for long periods in prison. It does not make sense to take youth who are prepared to risk their own lives in this way and to punish them when there are so many sensible recommendations as to how to avoid these problems in the first place. Just imagine what would come of adopting the Blue Print to stop bullying or the good sense recommendations from the NAAG.

INVEST IN KEEPING YOUTH IN THE COMMUNITY

The knowledge available goes beyond what has been shown to reduce crime and victimization. We also have some useful information about the comparative costs and benefits of different strategies, and some of this information is being used to decide large investments by governments in strategies to reduce crime.

In the 1980s, one of the examples that I used frequently to illustrate that an investment in prevention provided benefits in terms of crime reduction and payment of taxes was Job Corps. Job Corps succeeded by providing job training to high-risk youth in making a job more attractive than crime. It included a residential environment that helped provide social and educational supports for the youth.[8] Although the benefits were not large, they occurred in a large-scale program of the U.S. Department of Labor, designed to provide job training and social support to at-risk youth so that they get and keep jobs. The number of youth passing through the program is important, as political elites would be right to be cautious on projects with small samples even if the effect on crime is proportionately large.

The group of criminologists at the University of Maryland described Job Corps as their poster child because it reduced crime in the way that they thought tackling unemployment would reduce crime. Since then Job Corps has been subject to a more up-to-date evaluation, showing that high-risk youth get jobs from the program and are 15 percent less involved in crime.[9] Given the overall benefits of the program, it is undoubtedly an important one to pursue. The analysis of the reasons for the drop in violent crime in the 1990s also points to jobs being created for unskilled workers, particularly when the rewards from illicit markets were also reduced.[10]

Another success story that earned the title of a Blue Print Model Program focused on families that have a youth at risk. James Alexander, a psychology professor, and Bruce Parsons, a social work professor at the University of Utah, realized thirty years ago that it was not sufficient to work with just the youth at risk, but that reductions in offending and other problem behaviors required work with the family. In the intervening years, a systematic approach has been developed that includes systematic training of therapists, supervision of the therapists, and assessment of the results that they are able to obtain. Although the name of the approach—Functional Family Therapy—sounds complicated, the results are impressive. The program starts by helping the youth and their families identify a sense of being able to improve situations. It then uses this to identify how the youth and the family can change their situation. It also helps the youth and the family to sustain the change. The program can be completed within a ninety-day period, including ten to twenty hours of direct service costing between $1,000 and $4,000. When the proportion of youth arrested who have gone through the program is compared with the proportion arrested in a comparison group in clinical trials, scientists are able to demonstrate reductions that are upward of 25 percent. These are particularly impressive because there have been more than thirteen separate clinical trials. In some the reductions have reached 60 percent. Like most of these preventive blueprints, the programs are also extraordinarily cost-effective. Recent comparisons of the costs of the program show that it is possible to deliver it for as little as $1,000 per family in the community compared to a cost from $6,000 to $13,500 in residential prison programs. For this low cost, it is also able to get a 50 percent lower arrest rate than the standard ways of dealing with these youth. WSIPP showed that Function Family Therapy showed a return of $20 in reduced offender and victim costs for every dollar.

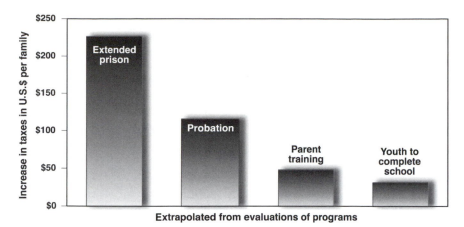

Figure 2.1. To achieve a 10 percent reduction in crime, what increases in taxes are needed using incarceration, probation, parent training, and school completion.

Andrew Karmen is the New York sociology professor who undertook the only comprehensive analysis of the true reasons for the reduction in crime in New York City in the 1990s. He identified four factors that he showed to be particularly important in explaining the reduction. One of these is alcohol use, which we will examine in the next chapter. Another is the proportion of families with strong family and work values, particularly with new immigrants. This is consistent with what has already been said about completing school, job training, and getting work. He concluded that the job market is particularly important in reducing crime, particularly if it pays salaries that make illicit activities less interesting. This is very much consistent with my conclusions on Job Corps. He also stressed that getting more young men to go to college reduces crime. In the case of New York City, that happened independently of a crime prevention intervention but he would want us to look at what can be done to increase enrollments in colleges because they provide better access to so many experiences that improve one's life chances.[11]

At the International Centre for Prevention of Crime in the 1990s, we developed a diagram (Figure 2.1) to communicate to governments the financial advantages of particular crime prevention through social development. I have used this successfully with several government funding agencies, including the British Audit Commission, the South African Department of Finance, and the Canadian Treasury Board to persuade them to start investing in crime prevention. It shows the significant benefits of investing in crime prevention through social development over incarceration. It is based on data brought together by the Rand Corporation in California.[12] If a politician wanted to reduce crime by 10 percent in California, $220 of taxes paid by the average family would have to be used to achieve this objective through incarceration. In contrast the same goal could be achieved by spending $45 of taxes for the average family on better parent training for young families or for only $30 of taxes per family to help kids at risk complete school. In sum, it costs taxpayers seven times as much to reduce crime through incarceration as it does through promoting school completion.

Much of this knowledge is ignored by politicians in making decisions on budgets. Judges in juvenile and criminal courts do not have to consider these budgeting issues when they take decisions on whether a convicted offender should be sent to prison or to probation. Unlike doctors who have to check whether a bed is available in a hospital, judges do not have to check whether space is available for detention. Unlike doctors who must establish priorities on the use of expensive treatments, judges do not have to identify the offenders whose offenses were the most dangerous and serious to ensure that they will be incarcerated.

Many programs that are absorbing significant public resources in the name of crime reduction have not been evaluated. So there is a need to undertake much more extensive evaluation of the costs and benefits of programs. The Washington State Institute on Public Policy has already demonstrated that some common programs are known to be bad investments, producing increased recidivism, such as placing youth in "boot camps" where teenagers are treated like new army recruits or taking first offenders to maximum security prisoners to "scare them straight." Boot camps would lose $19,011 per participant. They call for resources from these programs to be reallocated to those that yield positive results.

LEGISLATE AN OFFICE TO STOP MISSPENDING ON YOUTH AT RISK

In 1996, the British Audit Commission published a report with the poignant title *Misspent Youth*. The report was an analysis of the returns that British taxpayers got from paying for standard police, courts, and corrections as the way to respond to young people and crime. The report concluded that resources could be used better because prevention is much better than cure. In sum, taxes are being misspent on running after youth in conflict with the law, and as a result youth's lives are being misspent. Offending is more likely following life experiences identified by the longitudinal studies such as troubled home life, including poor parenting, criminal family member, and violence of abuse. Also listed were peer group pressure, poor attainment at school, truancy and school exclusion, and mental illness or abuse of alcohol or other drugs and deprivation, such as poor housing or homelessness. The report made a number of recommendations as to how the money should be spent from assistance with parenting skills to support for teachers dealing with badly behaved pupils and positive leisure opportunities.

Just two years later, when the Blair government came to power in England and Wales, it acted to create a permanent Youth Justice Board (YJB) to act on the recommendations of the Audit Commission's report. The YJB has an independent board drawn from leaders in policing, social service, education, and so on. Originally it was chaired by Norman Warner, the policy adviser on crime to Blair when he was in opposition. It is now chaired by Rod Morgan—a criminologist who has combined a distinguished publication record on youth justice, criminology, detention, and so on with government experience as the chief inspector of probation, chair of a community safety partnership, and an activist to stop torture. The result is that England has leapt ahead of other countries in providing good youth justice but more importantly, it has multiplied successful "pre-crime" prevention programs across difficult neighborhoods.

The YJB has already cut delays between arrest and conviction in juvenile courts by half and has started programs achieving reductions in young offenders repeating offenses. It is committed to confronting young persons with the consequences of their acts, reparation to victims, and tackling risk factors in the family, housing, and school situations. It calls the latter "pre-crime" prevention, and its resources allocated to prevention are used to identify and promote various strategies that are known to be effective in reducing crime. This is done by controlling the quality of the work done with the funds. Similar programs in the United States and Canada and even the British Home Office just make funds available for communities to apply for. Not surprisingly, these funds are often not used very well to reduce crime. Instead, the YJB sets out to achieve specific goals relating to the reduction of youth offending. It also invests a portion of its funds toward the quality of implementation and the evaluation of its efforts in crime prevention.

The "Youth Inclusion Program" is a prime example of the YJB's knowledge-driven pre-crime prevention programs. For this national program, the YJB funded an independent group called Crime Concern with an impressive track record of successful implementation. It is Crime Concern that focused on the fifty most at-risk youth aged 13–16 in seventy of the most difficult neighborhoods in England and Wales. The youth are provided with ten hours a week of activities, including sports, training in information technology, mentoring, and help with literacy and numeracy issues. The program also includes assistance in dealing with violence, drugs, gangs, and personal health.

One of the YJB's goals is to achieve an overall 30 percent reduction in youth offending in at least two-thirds of the neighborhoods with a Youth Inclusion Program. The YJB set aside 8 percent of the Youth Inclusion Program costs to ensure the quality of its implementation, and 6 percent for the evaluation of the project nationwide. A preliminary evaluation of the Youth Inclusion Program reports an amazing 65 percent reduction in youth arrests, a 27 percent reduction in youth removed from schools, and a 16 percent reduction in overall crime. The Youth Inclusion Program clearly illustrates the reductions in crime and victimization that can result from the leadership of a governmental crime prevention responsibility center dedicated to effective practice. The program costs about $5,000 per place per year. Coincidentally, this is the cost of taking a young offender through the youth justice system for one offense.

The YJB used the results from the evaluation to expand the program to more than 100 neighborhoods and to start an equivalent program with youth aged 8–13. The YJB provides a powerful model for how to improve the way in which the government goes about its work. The purpose of the YJB is to ensure that departments and agencies at all levels implement effective action to prevent offending by children and young people.

IN CONCLUSION

The analysis of the longitudinal surveys confirmed that the propensity for young people to offend is increased by experiences such as inconsistent and uncaring parenting or dropping out of school. Further, their offending is more likely to become persistent the more they suffer from these types of negative life experiences.

Many small-scale projects and a few larger-scale programs have demonstrated that it is possible to tackle a particular risk factor so that children grow up to be less delinquent than expected. For instance, when we focus on young children at risk by providing enriched preschool programs or more public health nurses to help their mothers, we reduce the chance that the child will become a persistent delinquent in his or her teenage years as well as reduce child abuse. Also when we help youth at risk with mentors, assistance to complete school, or family functioning, they victimize less in their teenage years. Similarly, programs have reduced bullying and youth offending in the community.

The degree of success from these projects that focus on one risk factor at a time varies from 30 to 75 percent, and the programs are extraordinarily cost-effective with $4–$20 in benefits resulting from every dollar invested. But we also know that the more risk factors are present in a young person's life, the more likely the person is to be a persistent offender. So, the more likely we are able to muster a series of programs that tackle several risk factors, the more likely we are to get a larger reduction in victimization. It would seem reasonable to achieve a reduction of over 50 percent by using several of these effective programs. Just imagine what $100 billion invested in these programs would have achieved in crime reduction.

3

Outlaw Violence, Not Men

Violence that targets a young woman in her prime or occurs on a public transit system is in the headlines the next day. The media coverage of such events frightens millions of viewers. Many women will feel unable to go out alone. Transit system users will do so anxiously. Because the mass media report on the exceptional and sensational and let "what bleeds lead," this public violence dominates our images and fears about violence. Not the drive-by shooting, the high school student killing his peers, the sexual predator, or the London suicide bomber who perpetrates the most frequent or even the most devastating violence. It is parents and intimate partners committing violence behind closed doors that most often send loved ones to hospital or the morgue.

Violence is an everyday reality. Teenagers fight, sometimes in gangs. Parents abuse their kids. Spouses assault their partners. Persons sexually assault others. Kids bully others. People kill. The dominant fact about violence is that it is committed more often by men, in particular young men. When it happens behind closed doors, it is predominately against a woman.

But these are not the only dominant facts about violence. The political elite react to it rather than prevent it. They react with criminal laws designed to incarcerate its perpetrators—young men, often disadvantaged by race or birth. They miss the logic that young men who are prepared to risk their own lives in fights or shootings will not be deterred from violence by threats of incarceration and in some cases the death penalty. The political elite also overlook the need to solve the problems of violence behind closed doors.

The end result is that violence goes on victimizing young men, women, and children. People, particularly women, live with fear of a random attack. We as taxpayers pay for police and lawyers to incarcerate—outlaw—our young men. As we saw in Chapter 2, the prestigious commissions have concluded that violence will be reduced through more public health nurses, programs to help at-risk kids complete school, job training, youth centers, and so on. However, the public health doctors at the World Health Organization (WHO) have taken this a step further in their efforts to reduce injuries, fatalities, and trauma from violence. They stress that violence is not an accident, it is preventable. So our political elites must tackle the risk factors that make violence preventable.

WHO published a prestigious report on interpersonal violence, which for them includes violence among young people, child abuse, intimate partner violence, sexual violence, and abuse of the elderly.[1] They emphasized that violence is produced by social forces. So the solutions to the prevention of violence are to tackle those social risk factors. Although they see a role for law enforcement and criminal justice, it is by no means a central or exclusive role. They identified many of the risk factors that cause violence. Violence in our homes, schools, and our culture fosters young men who use violence as adults. Violence also flows from the availability of firearms, particularly hand-guns that may or may not protect but they certainly maim and kill. Violence is more likely when alcohol is easily available and consumed to excess.

In 2004, the public health doctors at WHO published another seminal report on fatalities and injuries on the road.[2] We lazily refer to these as accidents but WHO defines these as crashes because many of them can be put down to risk factors that can be influenced. In fact, many—not all— are similar to risk factors known to prestigious commissions as risk factors that cause interpersonal violence. In particular, the persons predominantly involved in the crashes are young males, some with similar backgrounds to property offenders, some being reckless, some drunk, and some with all of these. There are other factors, such as they drive vehicles that have not been designed to protect them in a crash.

OUTLAW VIOLENCE AGAINST WOMEN

Much of the physical and sexual violence against women occurs in intimate relationships. Some occur on the street and at places of employment. It must become a major priority in preventing crime because the impact of physical, sexual, and psychological harm on women is immense. The pain is just the tip of an iceberg, which includes persistent fear and anxiety, sexually transmitted diseases, pregnancy, or violence during pregnancy. It often results in persistent use of health services and difficulties in relationships and at work. In addition, violence by men on their female partner makes any children who witness it more likely to engage in violence later on.

The prestigious commissions have looked at what can be done to prevent violence against women but their conclusions are disappointing as they do not indicate any clear course of action. For instance, both WHO and the National Research Council comment on the lack of research on how to prevent violence against women.[3] They also note that the research that has been done focuses on law and order methods after the violence has occurred rather than on prevention of violence.

In the 1970s and 1980s, women's groups lobbied the mainly male political elites to take actions to prevent violence against women. The advocates wanted attention to the issue. Women lobbied successfully to redefine the offense of rape into sexual assault. The importance of clarifying that women are not chattels of their husband or father is undeniable. Also, emphasizing the element of violence is important, but I would also like to see both an emphasis and a recognition that violence is more often against women who are often more vulnerable to the violence. The emphasis on violence in sexual assault is also good, but the passion to use law rather than effective prevention is misplaced.

The feminists in the 1970s and 1980s launched refuges where battered women could go with their children to be safe from the man who was attacking them. Surprisingly, the effect of these refuges on violence against women has not been assessed scientifically. It seems to make sense that providing a safe haven to women might strengthen their ability to say no to violence and so protect them. Also the safe havens do indeed provide protection, and so there would be less repeat violence, which is part of this sad reality.

The advocates also argued that if we punish street violence with incarceration, then we should also punish domestic violence with incarceration— overlooking the fact that punishing street violence with incarceration only had a limited impact on street violence. Regardless, states passed laws that required police officers to arrest a suspect if they were called to an incident involving violence in a family. In 1984, one RCT scientific experiment in Minneapolis demonstrated a 50 percent reduction in violence by men who were arrested for assaulting their partner compared to those where the police officer responding to the call separated the couple temporarily or cautioned the man not to assault the spouse again. Quickly, states were passing similar laws. But replications of the scientific evaluation of these mandatory arrest procedures in other cities did not show that they were any better than warnings or counselling by a police officer. The conclusions flipped back and forth between making no difference and some difference. Eventually, it was concluded that there was little impact on men with little to lose—the typical offenders for whom incarceration is the usual and ineffective solution at the moment. However, there was some impact on men with something to lose— the typical middle-class men who are deterred by traffic laws. Even these experiments did not look at whether arrest and prison time were better than a requirement for an offender to take part in a specialized treatment group when his participation would avoid prison time.

One of the most interesting initiatives to assist women who are victims of violence in their home was developed in Brazil and not in North America or Europe. Police stations where only women worked were established so that ordinary women who were victims would have more confidence that they would be treated seriously when they went to the police station. In practice, these police stations also had doctors and psychologists available to the women so that they could get help with recovering from the violence and working out what to do with their lives. Like the North American refuges, these stations would be empowering to women and enable them to stop some of the violence. Unfortunately, police services in North America have resisted this type of initiative to stop violence against women. Also unfortunately, the researchers have not focused on this sensible option.

Efforts have been made to intervene with batterers by getting them to take part in group counselling designed to help them control their violence. There have been many scientific evaluations. The conclusions make disappointing sense. If the men stay in the programs long enough to get control of their violence, then they reduce violence but in most cases the men do not stay for that long. Surely it is possible to organize these so that men stay in the programs long enough.

So the actions to prevent violence against women are mostly after the fact and set in the law and order paradigm.[4] However, women themselves at the U.N. level have a more comprehensive and sensible view. The U.N. agenda to reduce violence against women includes empowering women and girls by reducing discriminatory practices, involving women in decision making, promoting education of women, fostering women's networking, and improving women's self-esteem. These are all preventive approaches that are as relevant in the United States as in Canada or England and Wales as well as elsewhere. While they do not advocate less law, they do advocate more order. There is even some encouraging research to support the good sense from the United Nations. In both Canada and the United States, the number of women murdered by intimate partners has dropped significantly in the last twenty years. Much of this has followed the general decline in murders. However, the decline has also coincided with an improvement in employment opportunities for women, liberalized divorce and child support provisions, and increased services for victims of domestic violence such as the refuges.

While I cannot demonstrate conclusions from prestigious commissions, it can be asserted that good sense would reduce one of the more horrific types of violence against women. These are the serial murders committed against prostitutes who work on the street. These include cases like that in Green River near Seattle or Vancouver, Canada, where in each case more than fifty women had been killed. These cases happen because men are able to pick up female prostitutes who work on the street and kill them, almost with impunity. These are written in the press as a growing number of women who disappear. Eventually the man is caught, tried, and sentenced to very long prison terms or even the death penalty. But the bottom line is that this will go on occurring with or without severe penalties until women who choose to work as prostitutes are provided with some protection.

The city of Amsterdam has accepted the world famous "red-light" districts. These are areas where women can work as prostitutes in rented shop windows. Usually this enables the woman to work as an independent entrepreneur. She does not have to step into the car of an unknown male. She is near other women whom she can call for help if necessary. She is near health assistance to avoid the spread of sexually transmitted diseases. In some Dutch cities, the women have to have a license from the municipality.

The advantage for Amsterdam is that this has become part of the tourist attractions for the city. So it brings in more tourists in hotels and restaurants. I have not been able to find research to confirm the assertions that this is safer, leads to less spread of sexually transmitted diseases, and so on, but good sense says that this is an inspiring example to look at. In 2006, the British government announced a new policy to deal with prostitution, including street prostitution. This followed several years of studies by their research group and a consultation paper. They did not choose the Dutch red-light-district approach but preferred an approach of allowing two or three women to share an apartment without soliciting on the street. Either model would reduce the serial murders of large numbers of women. Probably such models are long overdue in the Mexican border cities such as Juarez, where it is not 50 but 500 women who have been killed.

OUTLAW VIOLENT CONFLICT RESOLUTION

The good public health doctors at WHO like the bureaucrats at the United Nations call for educating our youth so that they know how to avoid instigating violence. For instance, the school curriculum could include programs to teach students how to resolve conflicts peacefully and a focus on understanding the differing perspectives of men and women in relation to violence and sexual assault. WHO also draws attention to programs such as the Canadian White Ribbon campaign that encourages men to show that they are against violence against women by wearing a white ribbon. Their slogan is that they are men working to end violence by men against women. They promote their campaign in schools.

I would like to be able to include recommendations from the prestigious commissions that programs to train youth and adults in peaceful conflict resolution reduced violence. Unfortunately, there is no research or recommendations to do this. However, there is no contrary research. Nevertheless, teaching youth how to negotiate and resolve disputes without resorting to violence makes good sense.

YOUCAN (Youth Organizing to Understand Conflict and Advocate Non-Violence) is a Canadian youth organization that has taken to heart the resolution of training youth in conflict. It goes into Canadian schools and has trained more than 16,000 children and youth in ways to resolve conflicts without recourse to violence. It is similar to the peer mediation programs that are used more widely in Canada and the United States. YOUCAN is an organization focused on training youth in conflict and on violence prevention. Its mission is to equip and inspire youth to peacefully resolve conflicts and develop healthy relationships in their communities. This for-youth-by-youth organization has developed eight core training modules in the area of mediation, peace circles, cross-cultural conflict resolution, Peer Helpers, Youth Taking Action, and so on.

The founders of the YOUCAN modeled their program to teach conflict resolution on programs to reduce drowning fatalities. They had noticed that many countries had succeeded in reducing drowning by teaching people how to swim and how to save life. So they decided to reduce violence by teaching people how to resolve disputes without violence and how to intervene to de-escalate violence. They go into schools and teach students how to listen actively and how to resolve disputes without using violence. They also provide training to young persons so that they can train others to do the same. This is similar to techniques that have been used in violent Latin American cities, such as Cali, with success.

This technique needs testing but it could lead not only to less violence between those at school but also to less violence in other settings such as the home. In the 1960s much of the awareness of the dangers of smoking tobacco was communicated through school programs that taught kids about the negative impact of smoking tobacco on health. The children brought this message home to their parents to remind them that they did not want to lose their parents, and so they wanted their parents to stop smoking. Similarly it is possible that if kids remind parents of the dangers of violence, then gradually more parents will seek other nonviolent ways to resolve conflict.

OUTLAW HANDGUNS

There is significant research on the role that handguns play in facilitating murders, robberies, and so on. The analysis of data from the International Crime Victim Survey in eleven countries confirms that the more guns in households, the higher the homicide rates. One interesting study by Dr. Sloan and his colleagues compared the homicide rates of Vancouver and Seattle that are generally comparable in terms of age, race, and income.[6] They pointed to a 50 percent higher homicide rate in Seattle because of greater availability of handguns.

My colleague at the University of Ottawa, Tom Gabor, has specialized in bringing these statistics together for Canada and the United States to show

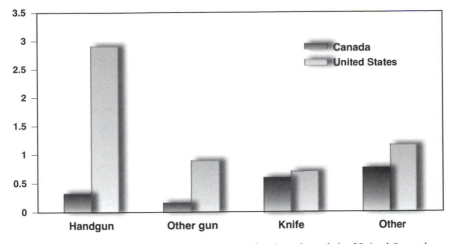

Figure 3.1. Rates of homicide per 100,000 for Canada and the United States by weapon used.

that the risk of being a victim of an attack in which a gun was involved is six times greater in the United States than in Canada (see Figure 3.1). In the United States, 28 percent of households have handguns, compared to 4 percent in Canada. Over 60 percent of homicides in the United States compared to 30 percent in Canada are firearm-related. Similarly 40 percent of robberies compared to 25 percent in Canada are firearm-related. In fact, the rates of murders without guns are similar in the two countries!

Bowling for Columbine—Michael Moore's Oscar-winning movie—glorifies the major difference between the United States and Canada in relation to guns and violence. In the United States, people own handguns to protect themselves. In Canada, people own long guns to hunt. This is in part the result of deliberate policy initiatives that have taken place in Canada, of which the most significant is the 1977 firearm control policy that was thought up by the research and statistics group for the Solicitor General of Canada. Essentially, this program banned automatic weapons, stopped persons from carrying guns for self-protection, and required hunters to have a certificate to acquire a firearm. The certificate was obtained in a process similar to obtaining a passport. It also encouraged owners to keep ammunition separate from the long guns.

In the United States, 67 percent of gun owners have them to protect themselves from crime, according to a Gallup Poll.[7] Good sense would lead me to believe that if we could prevent crime better, many owners would eventually be prepared to give up their guns because they would not need them. Canadians do not feel they need guns because there is less crime. So if the political elites would invest—even part of the $100 billion—into the proven or sensible prevention programs discussed in this book, it would reduce crime. By making the United States safer, it would also permit more Americans to live without the crutch of a handgun to protect them.

Even though the United States has resisted any form of gun control, law enforcement and police are aware that handguns and other firearms are used in a lot of crime. So they have been involved in a range of initiatives to get guns out of the wrong hands. Some of these actions have been the subject of scientific evaluations—RCT—designed to measure whether the police action to remove handguns reduced violent crime. The criminologists at the University of Maryland included this issue in their review for the U.S. Congress. Their conclusions are important. First, they have concluded that gun amnesties and buy-back programs do not reduce violent crime in the months following the programs unless they are targeted to high-crime areas.[8] The mayors are often persuaded by their police chief to establish these programs where the police accept guns handed in without any questions asked during a two- or three-week period. Some cities give a reward of $50 or so to the persons handing in the guns. The results overwhelmingly show no impact on violent crime, typically because the persons who hand in the guns are not those likely to use them in a crime.

However, when the police are smart and target seizures of illegal guns in high-crime areas, they succeed in reducing crime. The first scientific confirmation of this was the 1992 Kansas City Gun Experiment, which was replicated in Indianapolis in 1996.[9] It trained some of their police officers in ways to detect concealed weapons. These officers then used both traffic enforcement and field investigations to stop citizens in a high-crime area. Gun seizures increased by 60 percent and gun crimes dropped by 49 percent. In Boston, *operation cease-fire* focused police on using a range of enforcement procedures including traffic to seize guns and put persons persistently carrying guns behind bars. As we will see, the Boston action was accompanied by several other measures already discussed in Chapter 2.

OUTLAW DESTRUCTIVE DRIVING

One of the most ironical statistics for law and order professionals is that more people are killed driving cars than by handguns, knives, or any other object. It is ironic because we focus more attention on the homicides using handguns than we do on cars which are the most devastating killers.

The Centers for Disease Control (CDC) in Atlanta issues statistics on causes of death for the United States. In 2002, 44,000 people in the United States died in traffic crashes; 17,000 of those were killed in crashes involving drunk drivers. This was a significant drop in deaths from drunk driver crashes from 24,000 in 1980. The drop is similar to that for the murder rate which also dropped from about 25,000 in the 1980s to about 17,000 in 2003. The trends in homicide and drunken driving are following each other closely, because both are caused by the same trends such as fewer young men in the high-risk age groups, more jobs that pay a living wage, less abuse of alcohol, and more young people incarcerated.[10]

Mothers against Drunk Drivers (MADD) has fought hard and vociferously to get action to reduce the loss of life and the injuries from drinking and driving. Their mission is to "stop drunk driving, support the victims of this violent crime, and prevent underage drinking." In 1982, they got the president to establish a Presidential Commission on Drunk Driving, which recommended classic law and order proposals designed to punish drivers who were in charge of a vehicle with more than 0.10 percent alcohol in their blood. Others tackled risk factors through the use of interlock ignition systems that make it impossible for a person who is drunk to start that car or through the changes in drinking laws that increased the age at which someone could buy alcohol. Yet others were strategic as they tackled activities that increased the risk that drivers would use their vehicles when they had drunk too much, such as requiring servers in bars and restaurants to be trained so that they would not serve persons who were drunk.

The president's commission was followed by a permanent group called the National Commission against Drunk Driving, whose job it was to follow through and get action. Fortunately, MADD continued to lobby effectively at both the local and national levels. It continually drew attention to the numbers of persons killed and injured. They put a face on the people killed. Every few years, MADD does an assessment of progress made by the federal government and the states in taking action to reduce drunken driving fatalities along the lines of its recommendations. Its checklist is impressive because it focuses primarily on reductions in victimization—imagine a lobby group on gang shootings that uses a score card to measure whether the rate of shootings is going down. The checklist also focuses on whether the state has adopted the law and order proposals that MADD advocates. In 2002, it gave the United States a C+ score because there had been an increase in fatal victimizations compared to the year before. MADD called for a number of very sensible measures such as revoking driving licenses, measuring blood alcohol levels for all drivers in fatal crashes, and ignition interlock laws. It also calls for action to get drivers and passengers to use safety belts, generally recognized as the most important action to reduce death. Interestingly, MADD has been active on fighting for rights for victims, in particular to get amendments to constitutions, which we will discuss further in Chapter 6.

The CDC has a National Center for Injury Prevention and Control that has reviewed the literature on impaired driving. This evidence-based approach identifies a number of important ways to reduce death on the roads. It agrees with several of the MADD proposals because there is strong evidence that road deaths can be reduced through greater use of seat belts for adults and children and through programs that control alcohol impaired driving such as raising the minimum age for buying alcohol and reducing the legally acceptable blood alcohol level to 0.08 percent.

Some of the programs to reach the young adults who are most at risk of drinking and driving make good sense but have neither been the subject of clear evaluations nor the subject of significant funding. The program that makes the best sense is Students against Driving Drunk (SADD), which started in 1981 in Massachusetts. Robert Anastas was the hockey coach at a local high school in Wayland when two of his star players were killed in a drunken driving crash. This tragic loss was a call to action for him. He used his considerable abilities to reach youth to launch a national campaign to prevent youth from getting killed. As an educator and coach, he realized that the best way to help youth avoid drinking and driving was to get them involved in taking the decisions. He knew that the threat of punishment just like the threat of getting killed was not enough—a lesson that the political elite miss.

A key element in his strategy was a "contract for life." This contract required the teenager to think through and make a commitment not to drink and drive. He also got the teenagers to make the commitment to call a parent to get picked up if the teenager had drunk. The parent committed to pick up his or her son or daughter and not to discuss or punish the youth until the next morning. The parent undertook to call the youth to get him or her to pick up the parent to avoid driving after drinking. The good news is that this program has spread across the United States and other countries.

But there is more than what CDC or WHO recommends. In the city of Ottawa, Canada, they have adopted a three-pillar strategy that makes good sense even if they have not yet demonstrated its impact. This combines engineering to slow traffic through traffic calmers, education for drivers, particularly younger ones from public health nurses and drivers' training, and enforcement to keep drivers using seat belts, not driving destructively, and so on.

It is interesting to note that the prestigious commissions have overlooked the link between childhood experiences and driving behavior. We know that inconsistent and uncaring parenting, difficulties in school, and so on predispose youth to assaults and theft, but we do not know to what extent those same experiences predispose youth to drinking or other reckless driving. In the 1960s, a pioneer criminologist, Terence Willett, did a comparison of persons convicted of interpersonal crime with persons convicted of drunken driving and driving dangerously in England. This study demonstrated a close interconnection between the two.[11] That is, persons who are involved in interpersonal property crime are also involved in driving behavior, which puts them in conflict with the law. It is disappointing that those concerned with reducing deaths on the road have not pursued this connection further. In other words, if we implement the recommendations discussed in Chapter 2, we will also have an impact on fatalities and injuries on the road.

OUTLAW ALCOHOL ABUSE

Abuse of alcohol is well established as a risk factor that causes crime but the solutions are a lot less clear. The contrast between the United States and Europe is striking in the regulation of alcohol. In the United States, the drinking age is being put higher and higher—mostly as a result of pressure from groups such as MADD to bring down the death toll from traffic fatalities. In contrast, Europe allows alcohol consumption in teenage years and in some cases is liberalizing access to alcohol.

Nevertheless, the statistics confirm that drinking alcohol increases the likelihood of someone getting involved in violence. A high proportion of persons who commit offenses such as assault, sexual assault, violence against their partners, and murder are found to have consumed significant amounts of alcohol before the offense. The CDC is clear that heavy alcohol use is a significant risk factor in intimate partner violence. That is, those that consume a lot of alcohol and those who are actually drunk are much more likely to be both the perpetrators and the victims of this type of violence. The same is true for sexual violence. Despite their confidence in their knowledge of the risk factors, they do not provide examples of programs or projects that have targeted reductions in alcohol use as part of a strategy to reduce these crimes.

Although we know that increasing the legal age for buying alcohol has reduced traffic fatalities, it is less clear whether it is one of the reasons for the declines in rates of other common crime. Andrew Karmen in his analysis of the drop in crime in New York City points to the well-known positive correlation between trends in crime and consumption of alcoholic beverages—more alcohol, more crime.[12] In the case of New York City, he suggests that the decrease in the use of hard liquor like rum and vodka may explain some of the drop in crime. The successful efforts to reduce violence in Bogota, which we will discuss in Chapter 7, were associated with policies to limit access to alcohol.

Many cities face problems when young adults leave bars at the same time because a licensing law requires the bars to close at a certain time. The problems are in part issues of noise and disorder but there may also be fights as young males who are drunk bring their disputes onto the street. There may also be fights over access to public transit. Recently England and Wales has abolished a fixed closing time for pubs. This legislation allows pubs to stay open for as much as twenty-four hours in an effort to avoid the congestion in getting onto public transit. It has been accompanied in some cases by the creation of medically supervised clinics, where persons who have been binge drinking can recover or dry out. We will have to wait for the evaluations by the British government to see what effect this has.

Excessive consumption of alcohol during pregnancy can lead to children with the fetal alcohol syndrome, which is the name given to the damage to the unborn child from excessive alcohol consumption by a pregnant mother.

It leads to a number of mental deficiencies that limit the ability of the child to learn, which can increase their chance of committing crime. As there are no cures, prevention is important. The best prevention is information, education, and support for the mother to avoid drinking alcohol, but as most of the damage is done in the first three months of pregnancy, the mother may not be immediately aware that she is pregnant and may also have difficulty changing her habits.

OUTLAW DRUG WARS

If there was ever a battleground between truth and good sense on the one hand and the law and order industry on the other, it would be in relation to policies to tackle the trafficking and abuse of illicit drugs.

As the Drug Policy Alliance points out, the United States has spent $100 billion many times over in the last few decades in one or more wars on drugs. The main objective of these wars has been to cut off the supply of drugs to the U.S. market. They aim to stop farmers in impoverished countries from growing the basic ingredients; they use Rambo tactics to arrest and incarcerate the kingpin drug traffickers; they intercede in the supply chain as the drugs are moved from the producer country to the United States; and they enforce current laws against local gangs who distribute the drugs locally.

Unfortunately, the results are less than spectacular as drugs trade at lower prices than ever, meaning there are more of them. Heroin, cocaine, methamphetamine, crystal meth, and new and other varieties continue to be easily available in most U.S. cities and disturbingly in too many school yards. According to BJS, approximately 25 percent of all persons incarcerated in the United States committed their offenses to get drugs. So the reactive law and order stance is costing $42 billion a year if it is 25 percent of the total criminal justice costs of $167 billion. There is also a persistent debate about whether marijuana and its various derivatives should be freely sold, as in the coffee shops of Amsterdam, or whether its sale should be controlled by laws such as those that allow its use for medical purposes or the growth and sale of small amounts for personal use. For other drugs such as heroin and cocaine, the harm reduction strategy associated with the city of Frankfurt has become famous. Essentially, these try to stop the spread of AIDS and hepatitis C by providing free needles, so that users can shoot up the drugs with sterile needles. It can also include medically supervised clinics where users can go to shoot up the drugs in an environment where medical help is available to cope with overdoses and other complications. These strategies are about avoiding loss of life and spread of disease.

Too little attention is devoted to reducing demand, and the methods most talked about do not work. Drug abuse reduction education is one well-known program invented by the Los Angeles Police Department that sends uniform officers—the law and order industry—into schools to talk about drugs with the school kids. However, the work of Sherman and his colleagues at the University of Maryland shows that the evaluations of these programs have not been able to demonstrate any positive effect in terms of reduction of use.[13]

The city of Vancouver in Canada has made a reputation for its four-pillar approach to dealing with drugs. These pillars are harm reduction, prevention, intervention, and enforcement. They also want their action to be evidence-based. Just in ten years they have decreased the number of illicit drug deaths from 150 to 50, when the number of illicit drug deaths in the Province of British Columbia where Vancouver is the major city stayed constant at 150. This is dramatic proof of the effectiveness of a combination of tackling the risk factors that cause a crime problem through prevention and enforcement.[14]

The National Center on Addiction and Substance Abuse at Columbia University affirmed that parents who take a "hands-on" approach to their teenagers' lives substantially reduce the risk of those young people abusing drugs, alcohol, and tobacco. Moms and dads should be parents, not pals to their teenagers. The center reached this conclusion after undertaking a survey of 1,000 American teens aged 12–17. "Hands-on" referred to parents who took an interest in their child by monitoring what teens watch on TV or Internet, knowing where they are after school, being very aware of academic performance, and so on. The research is not strong enough to justify large investments but it makes good sense, and the costs are low.

In contrast, the University of Colorado at Boulder has included two Blue Prints to reduce violence, which focus on tackling the abuse of alcohol and other drugs.[15] These have strong research to support their conclusions. These are projects where an independent scientific evaluation has shown that they produce reductions in drug use and violence. In one project, known as the Midwestern Project, the aim was to avoid drug abuse from primary to secondary school by training students in life skills and providing information and skills to avoid drug use. It works with parent, school, media, community organization, and health policy to reduce adolescent drug use. The second project is known as Towards No Drug Abuse—the aim and methods are similar. It has been tested on 3,000 youth from forty-two schools. Its twelve classroom-based lessons are covered in a four-week period and include everything from discussion of the health consequences of drug use through communication skills to stress management. These programs achieve between 20 and 40 percent reductions in drug use. The costs to help 1,000 adolescents with drug abuse prevention through the Midwestern Project were $175,000—equivalent to the annual costs of two police officers.

Think what using the $42 billion spent on law enforcement and incarceration to react to drug abuse could do to reducing demand for drugs.

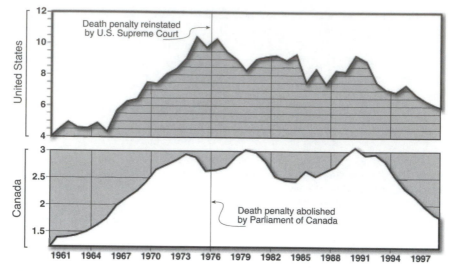

Figure 3.2. Rates of homicide per 100,000 for Canada and the United States with year of death penalty change.

OUTLAW DEATH PENALTY TO STOP KILLING

In 2004, 59 inmates were executed in the United States and 3,374 inmates were held on death row. Thirty-eight states and the federal government still have the death penalty as a sanction for murder. What will be surprising and disappointing to some is that rates of homicide are unaffected by whether capital punishment is used or not. For instance, the rate of decline in rates of homicide in the United States has been similar to that in Canada since 1976, when the United States reinstated the use of the death penalty and Canada took it out of its criminal code. For the period from 1968 to 1976, the U.S. Supreme Court stopped the use of death penalty in the United States because the statutes allowed its use in a manner that criminologists and others had demonstrated was racially biased—mostly that blacks killing whites were much more likely to be executed than whites killing blacks.

From 1976 until today, the homicide rate per 100,000 in the United States has declined from a peak of nearly 10 per 100,000 to close to 5 per 100,000 (see Figure 3.2). This is good news but not brought about by the use of the death penalty. Although the U.S. rate is more than twice that of Canada, they have both been declining at a similar rate. Many U.S. states have abolished the death penalty, and the U.S. Supreme Court has taken two recent decisions to stop the use of the death penalty for offenders who had a mental disorder or were under age 18 at the time of the offense.

No country can be a member of the European Union if they use the death penalty to punish criminals—killing offenders in a vane effort to stop killing.

According to the work of the British Home Office, the rates of homicide per 100,000 population have been relatively stable between 1 and 2 per 100,000 in Europe. The European Union has outlawed the death penalty. In practice, countries such as Turkey who want to join the European Union have to first abolish the death penalty.

IN CONCLUSION

Violence is not an accident, it is preventable. In Chapter 2, we have already seen the range of some Blue Prints that would prevent violence, including violence against children. To stop violence against women, there are promising tracks such as better employment opportunities for women, liberalized divorce and child support provisions, and increased services for victims of domestic violence such as the refuges. Hopeful programs would teach peaceful conflict resolution and respect between genders, particularly to schoolchildren, as well as provide victims with access to female police officers and counselors.

A major correlate of violence in the United States is the use of handguns, which is part of a vicious circle because people own handguns for protection as current law and order is not effective at preventing violence. However, when police remove handguns from the wrong hands, gun crime does go down.

Many lives would be saved through the use of seat belts and if programs endorsed by MADD were implemented, and also if more could be done to reduce driving that is destructive because of alcohol and other risk taking. We need to reduce the impact of alcohol consumption on crime, including preventing fetal alcohol syndrome. Let's use more of the truth in preventing drug abuse by reallocating significant amounts of the funds wasted on supply reduction to proven Blue Prints that reduce demand. Let's learn from the four-pillar strategies of Vancouver, Canada, to combine prevention and enforcement.

Once again we see an extensive list of programs that would prevent crime. Imagine what a difference $100 billion would have made to these.

4

Watch Out for Your Own Where Needed

On September 11, 2001, "Little Brother" was watching and recording on closed circuit television (CCTV) at the airports in the United States where Mohamed Atta and his group started their journey to hijack four aircraft, kill 3,000 people, injure and traumatize many others, and scare a nation. CCTV did not prevent their doing it. It did permit investigators after the fact to know where the terrorists boarded the planes and to establish their identities. On July 7, 2005, "Little Brother" was watching in England when four suicide bombers talked to a fifth man before boarding a train to go to the center of London. This was not enough to stop them blowing up three trains and a bus, killing fifty-six people, injuring and traumatizing many others, and scaring the nation. However, it did assist investigators after the fact to piece together how the bombers entered the public transit system and who they were.

CCTV is just one of the technologies sold on the grounds that it will lower crime rates by increasing the perceived risk to potential offenders. The theory is simple. Offenders will not commit offenses when their actions will be recorded on CCTV as they will be readily identifiable and so caught and convicted. While the theory seems plausible, the scientific evidence concludes that CCTV is not universally effective, neither are some of the other popular technologies. In fact as the terrorist examples show, CCTV is better at identifying who "dunnit" than in preventing them doing it.

The belief that crime could be reduced by tackling the opportunity rather than the offender has had a rich history. In 1961, in her *The Death and Life of Great American Cities*, Jane Jacobs drew attention to the importance of the number of "eyes on the street" where residents felt some ownership over an area. She asserted that the combination of eyes and ownership would reduce both property and violent crime on the street. This is one type of little brother watching out for their own. At that time, Oscar Newman—a Canadian-born architect who worked with the New York City Housing Authority—talked about "defensible space" that is designed into buildings so that the residents could watch out for persons approaching the residence and so casually defend their space. These were the visionaries in the 1960s that launched much of the public policy interest today in designing out crime.

But the evaluations of efforts to implement their ideas were not so encouraging. My own work on what prevents burglary in Toronto in the 1970s was just one of many that showed that these design factors were not as important as to know whether young men were growing up in situations that predisposed them to offending.[1] But my research did confirm that the presence of someone who did watch out was important in reducing burglary and certainly much more important than more police, prisons, and judges.

WATCHING WITH NEIGHBORS

Getting your neighbors to watch for you without Jane Jacobs' sense of ownership is generally even less effective despite the thousands of persons engaged in neighborhood watch across the world. Originally started as a way to prevent residential burglaries, Neighborhood Watch is the largest citizen movement for crime prevention. Despite its commitment to prevention and the numbers of persons involved, it is sadly not as effective as it could be— in part because it has become too much of a public relations arm for law enforcement and not enough a movement focused on reducing burglaries. Sherman and his colleagues at the University of Maryland conclude that the scientific evaluations of neighborhood watch as a way to reduce burglaries do not show it to be effective.[2]

However, the original program in the 1970s in Seattle known as the Community Crime Prevention Project that inspired neighborhood watch was successful. They confirmed scientifically that the program caused reductions of 50 percent in rates of residential burglaries, which were sustained for several years. These were authoritative results as the evaluation used a random control trial (RCT) by selecting the program areas at random from areas of high crime in the city so that a scientific comparison could be made between the areas with the program and those without. My analysis to identify the successful ingredients of the Seattle project points to the process of diagnosing the risk factors rather than the specific remedies such as better locks. It was successful because a municipal office diagnosed the problem to be solved before applying the solution. It cost money but prevention to be successful requires some investment—the ounce of prevention that is better than the pound of cure. The ounce was spent smartly.

The origins of the Seattle success story are interesting and as relevant today as they were in the 1970s. Shortly after his election, the mayor of Seattle set up a law and justice planning office reporting to him, not the police chief, and got this office to do an analysis of how much crime there was in the city, where it was located, and what were the causes—a strategy that, as we will see in Chapter 7, is the secret to successful crime reduction. This office also undertook some public opinion polls to check out what was disturbing the citizens of Seattle. The analysis was discussed with the heads of city agencies, including the police. Then it was submitted to City Council who endorsed the need to give priority to burglaries, sexual assaults, and robberies in small stores. At which point, the office started the second phase, which was to work out how to solve each of these three problems. They talked to experts, police officers, and social scientists and then came up with a solution tailored to each of these crimes—already less law and more order.

For burglary, they concluded—rightly or wrongly—that it was caused by residents who

1. left their homes without anyone present for long periods during the day and at weekends,
2. would not intervene when there were suspicious strangers in the neighborhood,
3. had not installed proper locks on their front doors, and
4. had not marked an identification number on property that was easily transportable and turned into cash such as televisions.

So they established the *community crime prevention* program—to remedy these deficiencies. It is important to note that the remedy targeted the risk factors that caused the crime—something that the National Research Council among many others sees as the secret to wise use of taxes to solve crime problems.[3] The U.S. federal government as part of its *Omnibus Crime Control and Safe Streets Act* of 1968 provided the city with funds for the program. Essentially the city—not the police nor some small nongovernmental group—hired a group of young university students whom they trained to go to the neighborhoods to convince neighbors to host small groups of their immediate neighbors to get to know each other and take precautions that would counter the identified causes. In other words, it created a community where one had been lost by urban living. The program included training on the following:

1. When and how to intervene if they saw someone who was suspicious, including getting agreement from their neighbors to confront the person and call police.
2. Ways to make their residences look as if someone was inside, such as using a dog or timers that turn radios and lights on and off.
3. What locks would be effective, such as dead bolt locks that are difficult to open with a plastic card.
4. Marking televisions, radios, and other easy transportable goods with their social security number.

Their analysis of what caused burglary was superficial but good enough to give hope for success. They also set up an independent evaluation of the program with the assistance of Dr. Matthews, a statistician. They agreed to deliver the program only in certain medium and high crime areas chosen at random. The evaluation used police records as well as victimization surveys to assess changes over time. The independent evaluation was sophisticated and scientific. Matthews declared that the program had reduced burglary by 50 percent or more in the target areas—an extraordinary success. It got an award from the U.S. Department of Justice as an exemplary program, and a manual was produced on how to implement it elsewhere.

Unfortunately, the evaluation was not able to pinpoint what made the program so successful. This, as we will see, would have been important in preventing the steady rise in the rate of burglaries. In a separate scientific analysis in Toronto, I was able to examine over 5,000 police records of burglaries and undertake a victimization survey on 1,500 households. I also interviewed a number of burglars to find out how they selected the residences that they entered. Putting the evaluation of the community crime prevention program in Seattle and the systematic analysis of the causes in Toronto together, it was clear that the active ingredients in the success of the Seattle community crime prevention program were the first two components; that is, the opportunity for burglary is created by a residence where an offender can approach it without being seen as they will not get caught, which is in part true. Burglars who think that there is no one around are able to go into a typical North American house in many different ways from the back, front, or side—so a one-inch dead-bolt lock on the front door is irrelevant.[4] Second, many of them are stealing easily transportable goods that they can sell on the schoolyard rather than worrying about the identifiers that would deter sales at a pawn broker or second-hand goods store.

My research in Toronto stressed the importance of human presence in preventing crime. Burglars reported that they did not want to confront someone. Therefore, they stayed away from residences where they thought someone was home. Our study showed that high-rise apartment buildings, having a concierge, never had a break-in. Whether the person is a concierge, family member, or paid security guard, the presence of any of these work to reduce residential burglary, and by extension many other property offenses.

Following the success of the Seattle program and the growing rates of residential burglary, citizens were clamoring for more effective programs. The manual for the community crime prevention program in Seattle was easy to follow, and it had pamphlets copy ready to be reproduced in other communities. It inspired the neighborhood watch movement that has spread across the United States and many other countries, with thousands of persons signing on for neighborhood watch. Almost everywhere I have been invited, there is an active neighborhood watch that gets its members— ardent believers in prevention—to turn out to hear me speak. Unfortunately, most get to hear that what they are doing as a neighborhood watch is not effective.[5]

What went wrong and what can these ardent supporters of prevention do? How could this succeed in Seattle but be a failure in most other cities? Regrettably those who wanted to adapt the program elsewhere did not take the time to read about how to analyze their crime problem so as to identify an effective solution. Instead they took the leaflets and the Seattle solutions and applied them as neighborhood or block watch in their city. Usually, they did not hire staff to make it happen or ensure that the meetings involved their immediate neighbors. They also did not target the areas where the program was needed as it was often the police department doing the program, whose men did not have time to go into neighborhoods that could not organize themselves.

Second, it was a movement run out of the law enforcement agencies that assign it to a low-level unit concerned with public relations, where the main interest of law enforcement is to improve public relations rather than achieve real reductions in crime. Too often the programs are organized in areas where there are residents at home during the day and able to take time to get organized—areas where the rates of burglaries are low.

Third, the spread of neighborhood watch has been achieved without paying for university students or other community workers to go out and organize the neighbors. If you want neighborhood watch to work, go out and do the problem analysis first to find out what is needed. Then expect to find a budget to pay for community workers to organize neighbors to solve the problems that the analysis will identify. Do not do it as part of a police department's public relations group. Interestingly the city of Montreal is one of the few cities that follow this advice. In the 1980s, it set up a remarkably successful community crime prevention program—Tandem Montreal—that remains a lonely but inspiring example today with a dedicated budget of several dollars per citizen from the city, which grows each year.

Meanwhile, the British began to be seriously interested in expanding crime prevention in the late 1980s. They developed a program similar to the original community crime prevention program in Seattle in the late 1980s in a residential area called Kirkholt near Manchester. They started with a diagnosis of the extent and the causes of residential burglary in Kirkholt, which was led by Ken Pease, a university professor, with a bent for inspiring people to think about solutions to what he has called repeat victimization.[6] His concept refers to the reality that many persons are victims of more than one offense in a year—often the same type of offense. In the case of burglary, he had noticed that many victims of burglary were victims again once the owner had had time to replace the stolen television or computer with a new one.

In Kirkholt, Pease inspired police, municipal officials, and probation officers to collaborate in the diagnosis. As they were involved from the beginning, they were keen to follow through with solutions. They faced an extraordinary high level of break-ins on a housing estate as well as a large number of burglaries which were repeat victimization. While the victims know that a burglar comes in more than once, the police often do not because they respond call by call rather than analyze the pattern of calls.

The team shared the knowledge that each had about who was committing the break-ins, in whose residences they were occurring, and what was being stolen. They then designed a response to each of these causes. They noted the extent to which cash in electricity meters was being stolen, and how little protection was provided by residents because they were absent or did not feel any responsibility for break-ins at residences of other persons. Therefore, they established a well-organized "cocoon" neighborhood watch, where the immediate neighbors were involved in collaborating and where the cash was removed from the residences. With the help of hired staff, they gathered neighbors and encouraged them to watch out for each other's property. Pease coined the term *cocoon neighborhood watch* to refer to the protection provided by having one's immediate neighbors watch out for one's property like the cocoon that surrounds the butterfly before it emerges.

They also improved the physical security of the area, such as by installing locks and lights and removing gas meters containing cash inside them which attracted offenders. The Kirkholt probation service was persuaded to provide high-risk offenders with more intensive rehabilitative programming. The result was a program that worked particularly with persistent offenders and repeat victims to achieve a 75 percent reduction in break-ins over a four-year period. They demonstrated $4 in savings in police time for every $1 spent on the program. Think what could be achieved by taking some of that $100 billion spent on law and order policing and targeting it to the analysis and implementation of programs like those winners from Seattle and Kirkholt!

Despite the impressive success of the program in Kirkholt, replications overlooked—as in the case of the imitators of the Seattle Community Crime Prevention Project—the importance of analyzing the problem before coming up with the solution. What works is problem solving. Replicating these, such as actions removing electric meters or whatever that had solved the problem in Kirkholt, for another city does not produce the same results. That is, the program will only succeed to the extent that it tackles a risk factor known to be related to the occurrence of the offense in your city or neighborhood.

WATCHING FOR YOUR OWN—PRIVATE SECURITY, ALARMS, OR NEIGHBORS

Today in the United States alone, there are at least 2 million persons employed in the private security industry whose annual operating expenditures will exceed $100 billion. Some of the private security agents are employees of big companies like retail stores or factories. Some are employees of private security companies that sell their services to rich individuals or companies. The key difference between the public police and private security is that those in private security work for the entity that pays them rather than in the public interest. Even so, some of these private security companies provide services to government such as protecting municipal buildings.

For every sworn police officer, there are probably three persons employed in private security. This is a remarkable reversal from the 1960s when there were twice as many sworn police officers as persons working in private security. I have shown the inexorable growth in public policing in the United States and elsewhere and the dramatic increase in the use of incarceration. The growth in private security is even more phenomenal. The growth is also remarkable because it reflects the lack of confidence of Americans in law and order. Despite the large increases in taxes to pay for more police, prisons, and judges, Americans are paying even more for more private security in greater numbers. Ironically, they also own handguns for the same reason.

The prestigious commissions have not commented on the effectiveness of private security in preventing crime. They do comment on the need to get better information on the size of the industry. Based on my research in Toronto, my perspective is that human presence and responsibility for protecting property should prevent crime against the owners of the property but not their neighbors.[7] So private security will often be a good investment in short-term protection. As most private security guards are not unionized or subject to the same controls as public law enforcement, they are usually cheaper than sworn police officers. There are measures that may be cheaper such as alert neighbors who have agreed to call the police, or a fierce watchdog who will scare off offenders. Nevertheless, paying for a private security service is probably a cost-effective way of providing protection to the rich who can afford private security should decrease crime, but only to the extent that they increase the effort needed to commit an offense or the risk of getting caught.

A large industry has also developed around alarms to protect both personal and commercial property. Some of these alarms are not connected to a central security firm but just make a noise when triggered. Some of them are connected to a central security firm who then makes simple checks with the owner to decide whether to call the police or fire services. Insurance companies will often provide a discount on insurance premiums to householders or business owners who have installed an alarm, presumably in the belief that this reduces burglaries.

The evidence on the real effectiveness of alarms is less clear. The authors of the International Crime Victimization Survey conclude that rates of burglary are marginally lower in residences where an alarm system is in place. For householders, the decision to use an alarm is less clear because the extensive installation of alarms has led to police being called to false alarms for which the householder may get fined. Again, I think the best alarm is one that is connected to an immediate neighbor who is present most of the time. So, immediate neighbors could provide effective prevention at very low cost.

In terms of preventing victimization, there is more to relationships with neighbors than watching out for offenders and protecting residences. Jacobs, in the 1960s, had already pointed to the importance of neighborhoods where people felt ownership. In the 1990s, Earls drew attention to how the feeling of ownership had contributed to lowering crime rates in neighborhoods in Chicago.[8] This finding came out of one of the largest criminological studies, costing more than $25 million. It was focused on following the development of children as they grew up to see what predisposed them to offending. He was able to conclude that the factors discussed in Chapter 2 were important but, in addition, the rate of offending was affected by the extent to which neighbors looked after their neighborhoods and intervened to deal with teenagers causing a disturbance or with persons selling drugs—what he dubbed "collective efficacy." His finding runs counter to the speculative view that police must tidy up broken windows. Instead of police doing the work, it calls for neighbors to take charge. This has many implications for public policy as it stresses that city planners must avoid breaking up cohesive neighborhoods and that investment in crime prevention must include efforts to encourage this collective efficacy.

WATCHING ON CAMERAS

Seattle was not only a pioneer of a successful neighborhood watch, its comprehensive citywide problem-solving approach in the 1970s led it to tackle robberies in small stores. Its office on law and justice planning concluded that the solution to these robberies was to place hidden cameras in stores to record the robbery and identify the culprit. Again with funds from the U.S. Department of Justice, it placed hidden cameras in small stores and asked the department's statistician to test whether it increased arrests. The conclusions were that it did not show a reduction in robberies but an increase in arrests. Remember that CCTV helps identify the offender after he has offended; it does not stop him from offending.

England and Wales are reputed to have pioneered the use of CCTV in public spaces as a law enforcement tool. They used them before the United States for a variety of purposes from video surveillance in their underground system in 1961, in shops in the mid-1960s, on roads in 1974, at soccer matches in 1975, and for public protests in 1984. Some other countries, too, had established a sophisticated travel control system using CCTV, such as Japan for Tokyo, in the 1970s.

It was hoped that the cameras in England and Wales would act as a deterrent to prevent crime rather than just help the police to know what had happened after the person was victimized. John Stevens, one of England's most distinguished and progressive police leaders was just one of many who claimed that a CCTV camera replaces the cost of keeping a police officer on a particular street corner, which requires more than twelve police officers to provide twenty-four-hour coverage for seven days a week. The police officer option would cost close to $1 million each year, substantially more than the few hundred dollars needed to place a camera and also monitor it. So it sounds like a good calculation to convince the political elite to use our taxes more smartly to reduce crime.

The British government has poured taxpayers' money into CCTV—hyperused CCTV like the U.S. hyperincarcerates. Yes, in other countries there are private sector CCTV in banks and shopping centers. There are also CCTV cameras at railway stations and airports, but Britain has invested millions of pounds in CCTV from the time of the Jamie Bulger case until today as part of a deliberate effort—albeit with limited success—to reduce crime. In 1993, two-year-old James Bulger was led away from his mother in a shopping center to his death. The two ten-year-old boys who took him were photographed on a CCTV camera in the shopping center. CCTV made it possible to watch the event on television and see photographs in the newspapers—all after the event had occurred. It is these tragic video clips that have stimulated the British government to invest significant sums of taxpayers' funds to multiply the number of CCTV cameras in public places. In 1994, the Conservative government invested 38 million pounds—$60 million. By 1996, more than 75 percent of crime prevention expenditures were on CCTV. In 1998, the Blair government allocated $500 million over three years to a crime reduction strategy that was based on its scientific analysis of what gives results. Then they added $220 million for CCTV even though the scientific information—the truth—did not justify any such investment. In the latest round, they invested over 150 million pounds or close to $300 million—about $6 for every man, woman, and child living in England and Wales! One group of researchers estimates that there may be 4 million CCTV cameras in public and private hands in England—one CCTV camera for every twelve people. The ones funded out of the public purse cover public spaces, back alleys, streets in difficult areas, and main thoroughfares. They have even reached the British countryside.

The scientific evaluations of the impact of CCTV on the prevention of crime show very limited results. Once again generalized use of CCTV has no impact, though CCTV targeted to particular parking lots or high-crime areas may give some success. This debate has been informed by scientific evaluations that started in the 1960s and 1970s with government experiments with CCTV in their subway in London to monitor platforms, in parking lots to prevent vehicle crime, and outside bars where there were frequent fights. The initial assessments showed these cameras were successful in helping police make arrests. In one major evaluation, they showed reductions in crime. Stevens introduced these into the center of Newcastle, a city of about 200,000 in northeastern England. CCTV was placed to provide discrete surveillance of troublesome nightlife areas, rapid response to incidents, and a record for use in court and to identify potential witnesses. Using a simple before and after comparison, a 56 percent reduction in burglary, 47 percent in vehicle crime, and 34 percent in criminal damage, and so up to a 19 percent reduction in overall crime was experienced.

However, two of the most famous experts on what works—Brandon Welsh of the University of Massachusetts and David Farrington of the University of Cambridge—completed a review of all this research for the British government in 2002.[9] They concluded that CCTV has only a small effect on overall crime reduction of about 4 percent, but it is more useful against thefts relating to cars and thefts on transit systems that do not involve violence. Evaluations of CCTV in town centers are much less clear. It does seem to increase the number of arrests for violence—fights—but little to reduce the number of victims.

WATCHING WITH CELL PHONES

Cell phones have become an important part of the crime prevention debate. On the one hand, they are stolen so often in countries like England that they have increased the rates of robberies in schools and on the streets. On the other hand, they have increased the opportunities for ordinary citizens to report events that they see. The addition of photo and video capacity has increased this yet further. We can now see the aftereffects of terrorist bombs because the victims have mobile phones with which they can record what is happening.

In England and Wales, a cell phone is stolen every three minutes. The phone may be worth $200 or more but the thief may be able to run up phone charges of several thousand dollars. Some thieves have cloned the cell phone identifiers onto their own cell phone so that an unsuspecting owner gets an extensive bill a week or more later. Cell phones have the advantage of being small, valuable, and easily transportable, which also makes them attractive items to steal. They can be sold on schoolyards and parking lots where sellers do not have to prove that the phones were not stolen. Given these characteristics, it is perhaps surprising that more have not been stolen. In part, there is a limit to the demand for the phones for those who would likely steal, sell, or buy on the street.

WATCHING OUT FOR OPPORTUNITY

Ron Clarke, once the head of the Home Office Research unit in the United Kingdom and now a professor of criminology at Rutgers University, has coined the term *Situational Crime Prevention* in his books.[10] He has brought together examples of crime prevention through environmental design (CPTED) as well as other measures that constitute situational crime prevention for him. Clarke has reduced the concepts to three central ideas. First, crime will be prevented to the extent that it is possible to increase the effort needed by the potential offender to commit the crime. Second, crime will be prevented to the extent that the risks of the offending getting caught are increased. Third, crime will be prevented to the extent that the rewards can be reduced. He has now added a fourth dimension that refers to spiking the arguments used by offenders as excuses for committing offenses. Although Clarke's categorization seems obvious, it is important to remember that the standard law enforcement and criminal justice approach is typically reacting to crimes one at a time and is not introducing protections such as these that reduce the likelihood of offending.

In 1961, Germany introduced a requirement for all new vehicles to be fitted with steering wheel ignition locks. An evaluation revealed that cars fitted with the ignition locks were stolen much less often than less desirable older models. This is one of the most successful national programs to reduce car theft. It is used as the prime example to show that when you increase the effort to commit a crime, you can reduce the number of crimes. The cynics suggested that this measure would just displace the crime from cars with the ignition lock to those without one, but the rates of car theft in Germany went down during a period when crime was generally increasing. A lot of car theft is in fact joyriding, where young persons take advantage of the availability of the car to have some fun driving it—the opportunity creates the crime. But such crimes are few in proportion to those committed by professional thieves, who will steal a car to sell the parts separately, which are in fact worth much more in the black market than the car in one piece. Indeed, this is the main limitation on much of these opportunity reduction techniques. They work well against occasional and amateur offenders. The professionals and those determined to achieve their illicit objectives will find ways around the protections.

For some large-scale programs such as the steering wheel locks, it is generally accepted that they work, though the proof is not scientific. Still others seem to displace crime without clear evidence of reduction. These are used widely by private security companies where displacement may be sufficient for them because they work for their employer rather than for the person against whom the victimization is deflected. They have costs to citizen's freedoms, but typically citizens will pay this price because they believe they are protected.

Nevertheless, Clarke's poster boy programs such as steering wheel locks and antihijacking searches have a dark side. They work for a time, but they may also result in much worse crimes. The car hijackings that take place in several developing countries and countries in transition, such as South Africa, show the limits of these strategies. In Gauteng Province, where I worked on national violence prevention strategies for two years, there were 6,000 car hijackings a year often resulting in death. The situational crime prevention techniques were very much present. Cars were fitted with steering wheel locks, car immobilizers, and even a system that gave electric shocks to anyone who touched the car. These forced persons who wanted to steal cars to use much more violent methods. So they resorted to commando raids on unsuspecting drivers when they were waiting at traffic lights.

While the German example was limited to reducing the opportunity by increasing the difficulty to commit the offense, today effective strategies to reduce car theft will be more comprehensive in as much as they will increase the difficulty to steal but also work on diverting potential offenders from wanting to steal. In the Province of Manitoba, Canada, a new strategy to reduce car thefts has succeeded in reducing rates by close to 50 percent. Their program includes a combination of subsidizing the placement of immobilizers in old cars and requiring new cars from 2007 on to be fitted with immobilizers, engaging citizens to help watch out for car theft, and programs for young offenders. The comprehensive strategy is being paid out of a premium on the auto insurance premiums.

The attacks on the World Trade Center also put in doubt the efficacy of the searches done on a universal basis at airports. Clarke claims that these checks stopped aircraft hijacking. Up to a point they did, but ultimately they forced the hijackers on September 11, 2001 to use a more organized and more violent method by taking over planes when they were flying and then guiding them into buildings. In terms of public policy, it is not clear what to do. Should one tolerate some of the less serious crime in order to avoid the worst or erect strong barriers knowing that eventually someone will do something far worse to get around the barrier. My opinion is that these techniques do provide some protection from the amateur and occasional offender, and so they are worth implementing. However, there is a danger of living in a fool's paradise as the techniques do not provide the 100 percent protection that their advocates claim. Its extensive use, for instance, to combat terrorism without some serious effort to tackle the causes of terrorism will only buy time before the professional and dedicated terrorists will find other ways of attacking. Once again we must balance law with order.

CPTED aims to design and use the built environment in a way that reduces opportunities for crime and lessens the fear of crime within communities. CPTED is a strategy commonly used by planners, architects, police services, security professionals, and so on. Examples of direct applications of CPTED include (but are not limited to) appropriate lighting in public spaces, visible entrances to businesses and private property, dead bolt locks, and peep holes on doors. In Canada, the skills of Patricia Brantingham have got CPTED concepts used in many different ways, including designing a whole new town—Tumbler Ridge—so that it had less crime.

Secure by Design is one inspiring example of CPTED for which research in the Netherlands has produced the evidence that it reduces residential burglaries. The initial program successfully reduced residential burglaries in Rotterdam, Leiden, and The Hague by setting standards for housing construction that reduced opportunity. Inspired by a little known British project, the Dutch police had developed standards that had to be met by new housing for it to be certified as safe. The police developed a manual on secure housing by design in order to help housing project developers render their homes unattractive to burglars. The manual covers areas such as parking, grounds, locks, entries, and resident participation and responsibility. In order to obtain the police label of approval on their housing projects, housing developers must meet the various specifications of the manual. All experimental programs in the Netherlands had to spend 10 percent of their funding on an evaluation. In *Secure by Design*, standards have been established for new residences so that they are less vulnerable to break-ins. The burglary rate for the new houses that met the standard was 50 percent lower than those that did not. This prompted the national implementation of the Secured Housing Label in 1996.

Improving lighting in public areas has been thought to provide some protection against crime. The review done for the Home Office by Welsh and Farrington agrees that improved lighting can in fact reduce crime.[11] They stress that the action must focus on a risk factor to be effective. The studies included actions to improve lighting in parking areas, residential neighborhoods, and local authority housing. In the right circumstances, improved street lighting can lead to a 20 percent reduction in crime in the area, which is important. The researchers also noticed that improved lighting seemed to go with communities where neighbors had got together to get organized—a factor known to be important from the work by Earls in Cicago mentioned in this chapter.

The principles of situational crime prevention and CPTED have important implications for industrial design. There is a need to establish standards in different industries that reduce the risk of victimization to the future owner of the product. The Dutch example illustrates how the construction industry was forced to design houses so that they were less at risk from break-ins. There is a potential for much greater involvement of experts on these preventive approaches to influence the design of everything—from cars to computers.

IN CONCLUSION

Watching over property has had some impact on reducing crime. Burglaries can be reduced much more by programs that are targeted to areas where they are needed and to risk factors identified as causing the problem. Volunteers may be adequate in some circumstances but the major reductions will come from professional staff hired by the city to achieve the reductions.

Private security and alarms that are connected to a live person provide some protection. A collective spirit in a neighborhood will prevent crime, and networks between neighbors with or without a joint alarm may provide better protection and less crime.

Despite the extraordinary expenditures by the British government, CCTV is better after the fact in identifying who did it than in preventing the crime in the first place, though there are some exceptions. Cell phones are as yet unproven. Crime can be prevented to some extent through the designing of housing and cars, though architecture alone is never sufficient.

The chances of sustained success will be increased by a combination of crime prevention through social development, as discussed in Chapter 2 and the measures identified here. Indeed, if the U.S. government had invested a fraction of what it spent on taxes on smart strategies like in the city of the Seattle, there would be many fewer victims today and many fewer young men for whom we have to pay their stay behind bars. Once again imagine what $100 billion could do to reduce victimization.

5

Police Smarter, Not More

In our lives, we see police officers drive past in a police vehicle, stop us for a traffic violation, or occasionally walk past us on a street corner. They make the presentations to the media on the latest murder or rape and celebrate the arrest of the culprit. On our television and movie screens, police are good-looking and tough heroes, committed to fighting evil international drug traffickers and vicious bank robbers. We often forget that we pay for them out of our taxes.

Their image has changed over the last forty years. The police used to be stereotyped in North America as overweight, corrupt, and occasionally brutal men. In the United Kingdom, their image was a friendly bobby epitomized in a TV series as Dixon of Dock Green who was a sympathetic father figure who solved disputes and helped kids in difficulty. Crooks were caught by detectives who befriended other crooks in bars. There was no national emergency number—911—no DNA and few forensic techniques. But all that has changed, as police management began to invest heavily in dispatch systems, radios, computers, and cars, particularly for random preventive police patrols.

Police leadership and police associations have changed the images. Professional organizations such as the International Association of Chiefs of Police and the Police Foundation have aided and abetted. Today, police and law enforcement are mostly well-paid professionals. Their resources have been shifted massively from walking beats into responding rapidly to 911 calls and coping with an avalanche of investigations. They have also had to deal with the massive increase in the number of cars on the road and consequent need to regulate everything from parking and speed limits to preventing drunken and dangerous driving. They have laptops in their cars and communicate with the latest technology through cell phones and radios. They are armed with handguns and Tasers—the electric stun gun, but not from "Star Wars." They like mission statements such as "to serve and protect" and make speeches about working with the community.

The change of policing into a profession has been dramatic. Many parents who wanted their children to grow up as lawyers now prefer their children to grow up to be police officers who are seen as stalwart and trustworthy citizens rather than lawyers whose image is not so good. Whatever their image, policing is big business in the United States with 1 million jobs, of which 800,000 are sworn police officers, and an annual turnover growing past $90 billion. In addition to the sworn police officers, BJS estimates that there are 250,000 civilians who work with police departments to look after a range of tasks that do not require a sworn officer. The average American family will pay $650 each year in taxes for this service—still only what it costs to install and monitor a popular home security system. This is one police officer for every 430 men, women, and children—maybe one for every 200 families.

A significant part of the growth was brought about by President Clinton in the 1990s, who promised to add 100,000 additional police officers. This was a 20 percent increase over the 500,000 at the beginning of his presidency. The Clinton increase was done by a standard "bait and trap" marketing method, where the federal government pays for the first few years when the salaries are low. The local government cannot resist the free gift. But it is a "pay later" scheme as the local government has to find the taxes for the salaries and benefits that are much higher when the raw recruits have been trained into fully operational police officers. The average expenditure per sworn police officer is closing in on $100,000. Ultimately, this is an increased burden on the local taxpayer, which may be justified if there is some additional benefit to the local taxpayer. However, we will see in this chapter that the benefit from more police officers is far from obvious, even though the public often respond to polls saying they would like more police.

Even so, 1 million persons working for policing seems like an army that should be able to fight crime. But policing in the United States is not so much an army as it is a multitude of 18,000 independent police agencies varying from a couple of police officers or sheriffs working for a small community to large agencies such as the Chicago Police Department with 13,000 sworn officers and the New York Police Department (NYPD) with a massive but fluctuating corps of 35,000–40,000 sworn police officers. The dispersion of policing into thousands of independent forces or services is not unique to the United States. It is similar in Canada, though two-thirds of their police officers are working for just five police services—two in the big cities of Toronto and Montreal, two provincial police services, and the federal RCMP. England and Wales has forty-three police agencies organized by region, including the London Metropolitan Police—Scotland Yard—with close to 31,000 sworn police officers. Note that London has many fewer police officers for a population only marginally smaller than New York City. One can say the organization of policing in England and Wales is more logical, though, as we will see, not necessarily more or less effective in reducing crime.

It seems a truism that police stop crime. We see them as the thin blue line that protects us from violence. They are somehow at the end of the 911 call that will save us in an emergency. Without thinking, we feel that they solve the crime problem when they catch their man—the murderer that we read about on the front pages of our newspaper. Our political elites think, feel, and talk the same way. They do not question whether extra police do, in fact, prevent crime. They would like to increase the number of police because they think it would make their voters happier, particularly if it can be done without the voters realizing that they will pay more taxes for this increase. The public relations machines of Giuliani and Bratton have fed these feelings. Indeed Mayor Bloomberg who succeeded Giuliani has continued the spin that the continuous drop in rates of crime in New York City is the work of the NYPD. Yet the truth is not so simple.

PUTTING POLICE WORK ON TRIAL

Do more police stop crime? Are they really the thin blue line between us and violence? Does their presence on a street corner make a difference? Do their investigations protect us? Did Giuliani or Bratton really deliver those large reductions that the media eulogize? Did Paul Evans make a difference in Boston? Do police provide value for our taxes?

If we had a police officer by our side, twenty-four hours a day, seven days a week, it would protect us from most crimes, but this requires nearly six officers just to cover the six thirty-hour shifts (calculate twenty-four hours for seven days divided by thirty). In addition they need holidays, training, sick days, and so on. When a strike by police unions leaves no police, several predatory crimes such as robberies and assaults increase. But this chapter is not about unrealistic extremes of employing every able bodied person to join the police or abolishing the public police. Instead it is about whether plausible increases in the number of police are a cost-effective expenditure to reduce crime. For instance, is there evidence to justify taxes being used to increase the number of police officers by 5 or 10 percent? Is there evidence that crime is lower because of the 20 percent increase in sworn police officers started by the Clinton administration?

In the last thirty years, some knowledge has accumulated that should inform our decisions as to how much to pay for policing and what to expect from those expenditures. Some of this knowledge comes from large-scale experiments—RCT—to test basic issues such as whether police patrols deter crime. Some comes from analyses and evaluations of other innovations. Some comes indirectly from the post hoc debate over the extent to which the crash in the rates of recorded crime in New York City was due to tough and more policing. But we also have to be careful about what has not been covered by the scientists, in particular the extent to which the public that is victimized by crime has (lost) confidence in the police.

Although different police chiefs describe their policing strategy in different terms, their resources are predominantly used in a reactive strategy or what the National Research Council called in 2004 a "standard" strategy.[1] This is the reliance across the board on random patrol, rapid response to calls for service, follow-up investigations by detectives, and unfocused enforcement efforts. Most of the police officers at the local level—65 percent or more—are used in patrol cars that respond to the ubiquitous 911 emergency number—usually to nonemergency and often not even criminal events. Another group—maybe 20 percent—works as detectives who largely prepare files to prosecute offenders already known.

In contrast, our images often come from Hollywood's fantasy world of police who perform miracles. In *Minority Report*, movie star police used sophisticated technology to identify who would murder next and where. Unfortunately, Hollywood is just that—a fantasy. Another romantic image in the media is that of detectives who work on "who dunnit" techniques worthy of Sherlock Holmes or Colombo. Nothing could be further from the truth. Most crimes that are solved, solve themselves. Not surprisingly as crime rates increased in the 1960s and 1970s, budgets for police could not be increased in proportion. As a consequence, the number of detectives available per crime has shrunk, so that they only have the time to investigate the most sensational and exceptional offenses.

The National Research Council reviewed the studies of the relationship between the number of police officers and levels of crime to conclude that most research shows that increasing the number of police does not decrease crime.[2] Their review included only one econometric study that found some positive relationship between increases in policing and decreases in crime at election time, which they dismissed as elections bring in new police chiefs and so different styles in policing. In contrast, I dismiss them because they use the number of crimes recorded by the police, which is notoriously related to discretionary decisions made by the police.

I also looked unscientifically at the percentage of reductions in crime levels in cities in the United States in the 1990s and was unable to find any obvious pattern. Some police agencies increased their complement by as much as 50 percent and some such as Washington, D.C., decreased their complement by 23 percent. In all cases the crime rates came down by 50 percent or more. If the number of police does indeed have an impact, it is not obvious and certainly does not justify large increases in our taxes, particularly when we look at other ways of reducing crime.

The bottom line from the National Research Council on several decades of research is that there is only weak or mixed evidence that the standard model reduces crime. Yet the debate among the political elite assumes that more police is better. In contrast, the National Research Council points to a body of carefully conducted research that provides much evidence of the effectiveness of the focused model of policing—what I call smarter policing. In sum, more is not better but smarter is.[3]

Another persuasive review of all this research comes from the prestigious board in England and Wales that oversees policing. It enjoys the quaint title of Her Majesty's Inspectorate of Constabulary (HMIC). HMIC is in fact made up of the cream of British police chiefs, who monitor and evaluate police work in England and Wales. In 1998, they published their own evaluation of the extent to which police made a difference to crime.[4] Like the National Research Council, they reached the somber conclusion that there is little evidence to support the contention that standard police practices reduce crime. This is an assessment of police effectiveness by the police themselves. So their conclusions on the limits of policing are particularly persuasive. If they have doubts as they do, then we should have major doubts about whether we are getting value for money—indeed any value in terms of crime reduction. However, like the National Research Council, they point out evidence that police can be effective if they use their resources in a smarter way. They are effective in reducing crime, and so provide some value for money when they are "problem-oriented"—that is, they tackle a particular risk factor such as taking away illegal handguns to reduce murders or stopping drunk drivers to reduce fatal car crashes. Similarly, they note the effectiveness of policing that focuses on hotspots—places where a lot of different crimes occur—or partner with an agency such as a school board that can tackle one or more risk factors such as those discussed in Chapter 2.

The standard way of policing represents massive spending. If 65 percent of the expenditures is used in responding to 911, as the National Research Council asserts, then taxpayers will spend $60 billion a year on this activity alone in 2006—rising to $74 billion by 2010. This is a staggering price tag. Similarly if 20 percent is spent on the investigative function, then $13 billion is spent on this annually.

Several small-budget items are the icing because they make police more visible to ordinary citizens and schoolchildren. In the name of what they call crime prevention, police have talked at neighborhood watch meetings, yet these were not effective as shown by the evaluations in Chapter 3. Instead, professional community organizers were much more successful than police in reducing burglary as in Seattle in the 1970s or Kirkholt in England in the 1980s. In the name of crime prevention, the police have a presence in schools as liaison officers and lecturers to promote drug abuse reduction education, only to find that the independent scientific evaluations have not confirmed that these activities have any impact on reducing crime. Even if they had reduced drug abuse, one can only wonder whether it would not be more cost-effective to pay professional teachers to undertake these tasks.[5] They have opened storefront police stations in the name of community policing, for which evaluations also show little impact in terms of crime reduction.

However, there is another sector of police departments that has been overlooked by researchers. That is the sector concerned with traffic enforcement, where the research was more positive on the effect of their strategies on reducing fatalities, injuries, and property damage. They enforce traffic rules and regulations—typically seat belts, speeding, drinking and driving, and not stopping at red lights. Despite the large number of deaths and injuries from traffic crime, the National Research Council was not able to report on much research about the effectiveness of these strategies in reducing fatalities and injuries. Other research suggests that police action to force road users to wear seat belts, not drink underage, and maintain their vehicle in working condition does in fact save many lives.

George Kelling, now a professor of criminology at Rutgers University in New Jersey, has played a significant role in the research on the effectiveness of policing and is often associated with the policies of Giuliani and Bratton in New York City. Kelling started his college studies in theology and then turned to social work for his postgraduate degree. When the Ford Foundation gave $30 million to start the Police Foundation in Washington, D.C., in the 1970s, Kelling was one of the leading researchers. He began his research on an influential experiment in Kansas City, Missouri, where the chief of police organized a special scientific trial—RCT—to test the effectiveness of preventive police patrols.

Kelling was in charge of the scientific trial. They decided to evaluate whether random police patrol did indeed prevent crime by deterring persons from offending. Random patrols are those where the police officers drive a car around a neighborhood without any specific target in mind except to leave the impression that a police car could appear at any moment to catch an offender in the act. The scientific trial was done systematically as an experiment. In some areas decided by the researchers, they deliberately withdrew preventive patrol for the twelve months of the experiment. In other areas, they doubled the number of patrols. In other areas, they left the number of patrols at the standard level. The public was not informed about the changes in levels of patrol. Kelling and his team then assessed whether there were any changes in rates of crime as determined independently by crime victimization surveys of the residents. These were done at the beginning and at the end of the twelve months. These measured the proportion of the residents who were victims of crime regardless of whether the victimization was reported to the police or recorded by the police. They concluded that the level of preventive police patrol had no impact on crime levels—that is, it did not prevent crime. Also the public did not notice the changes in levels of policing.

This was a dramatic indictment of the way the majority of police resources were being used at that time in the United States and many other countries. There was enormous resistance to the findings from police leaders and politicians because of the huge investment in preventive police patrols. Today we do not know what proportion of the resources of police services is devoted to random patrol.

It was this pioneering study that slowly led to diverting these police patrols from prevention to reaction to 911 calls, where 65 percent of local police resources are still spent today—$44 billion. This is not necessarily an improvement in terms of benefits to the public. However, it also led to some positive innovations that did give the public value for their taxes. The most important is called problem-oriented policing because it looks at the risk factors that create the crime problem. Once the risk factors are identified, the police uses its resources in a smarter way to tackle those risk factors and so reduce crime. The concept is ascribed to a Wisconsin University professor, Herman Goldstein.

One of the original examples of problem solving by a police department occurred in Newport News, Virginia, in the early 1980s. Essentially an enlightened police chief set aside twenty of his officers to analyze an area of the city where there were many break-ins, car thefts, and prostitution. Their job was to come up with a solution. In sum, they recommended that the city enforce its by-laws to improve physical environment issues such as lighting and the quality of doors in the housing estate. The end result was a reduction of 30 percent in burglaries.

In the United States, an office within the U.S. Department of Justice called the Community Oriented Policing Service (COPS) was set up with the Clinton administration's program to get 100,000 additional officers on the streets. COPS had significant funds during the Clinton period but this was cut by 80 percent by the Bush administration. Nevertheless, it continues to provide support and even some vision to policing in the United States. It defined community policing as "a policing philosophy that promotes and supports organizational strategies to address the causes and reduce the fear of crime and social disorder through problem-solving tactics and police–community partnerships." This is not bad for a policy statement, though it wreaks more of pleasing everyone than pushing what will really reduce victimization. Unfortunately, much of the community policing debate focuses more on police–community communication that makes little difference to crime than on addressing the causes or risk factors of crime through problem solving that does.

There is now an important Web site on problem-oriented policing that provides numerous other examples of crime that has been reduced by problem-oriented policing.[6] Some of the work of this site is influenced by the work of Clarke and one of his colleagues Felson, mentioned in Chapter 4. However, most of the examples are localized efforts by one or two police officers rather than citywide efforts to reduce crime.

For our taxes to be better used to reduce crime, we need smarter police departments, not just smarter police officers. We will now look at New York

City because of its reputation for miracles by Giuliani providing tougher
and more law enforcement. We will then look at Boston and its reputation
for having produced real results for two consecutive years by eliminating
murders with guns by persons under age 16. Then we will look at Chicago
where community policing was the model that was evaluated to show what
could be achieved in some neighborhoods.

Smarter Policing, Not More, Gave Marginal Returns in New York

In Chapter 1, the BJS data was used to show that violent crime crashed across the United States in the 1990s. Most of the crime reduction in New York
was just part of those national trends. So the question here is to assess what
difference, if any, Giuliani made to the drop in crime rates in New York City.

In the 1960s in the United States, crime and violence in cities like New
York were so bad that there was a presidential commission to find solutions.
Then there were two decades when the crime problem got even worse. So
history was made in the 1990s when the rates of violent and property crime
recorded by the police started coming down in New York City and then
reduced by more than 60 percent. These are all the more remarkable because they occurred in the largest city in the United States with 8 million
residents and about twice that number using it for work or play each day.
The scale of the change is illustrated more forcefully by the absolute reductions. In 1990—one of the peak years—there were more than 2,200 murders,
100,000 robberies, and 120,000 burglaries recorded by the police in New
York City. In 1999, there were only 671 murders, 36,000 robberies, and
40,000 burglaries recorded even though the population had remained relatively stable. While the 1999 figures would be scary to any person living
in a city in England or Canada, the decline in the rates of violence deserves
recognition and applause.

The media hyped this New York miracle. They reported that the crime
reductions were brought about by putting more police on the streets and
a law enforcement strategy focused on "zero tolerance" of petty offenses
and clearing up "Broken Windows." The police strategy was portrayed as
stopping people for petty offenses such as jumping turnstiles without paying
public transit fares, jaywalking, and urinating in public. The Broken Windows
work was focused on clearing up garbage and encouraging residents to take
back their neighborhoods. The media glorified the leadership of Giuliani
who started as mayor in 1994 and pillaged experts who cast any doubts as
to whether the drop was due to anything other than Giuliani's demands for
tough and accountable policing.[7]

The U.S. public relations machine has spread a message across the world
that Giuliani organized a miracle. Everywhere in the world I go, I am met
by politicians, public safety policymakers, senior law enforcement officers,
lawyers, criminal justice professionals, and ordinary people, all of whom know

the name Giuliani and are sure that he single-handedly brought the crime rate down by expanding the police force and using strategies known as "zero tolerance" because they were tough on petty offenses and "broken windows" because they repaired damaged property and cleared up abandoned cars and garbage. Some of them have traveled to New York City to see the results of the miracle firsthand. In addition to hearing from the police, they are able to walk around areas of New York City that have been transformed into fresh new high rise—the clear results of urban renewal rather than repressive policing. Then they go home assuming that they need to increase the police strength and engage in zero-tolerance policing to get the crime rates in their cities to come tumbling down. Unfortunately, they will not come down by anything close to the New York and U.S. national percentages unless they were due to come down for independent reasons.

The gullibility of world public opinion is as staggering as the drops in crime and violence themselves. Never do the media or the public relations specialists in New York City point out that history was also made in every other major city in the United States. The rate of violent crime as measured by the U.S. Department of Justice came down by 55 percent across the United States in the 1990s, as we saw in Chapter 1, and continued coming down until today—not just in New York City. It is clear that the majority of the declines in New York City were part of a general trend in the United States.

The media neither point out that a significant part of the decline in police-recorded crimes in New York City had occurred before the zero tolerance and Broken Windows strategies were introduced. That is, the declines started long before Giuliani was even elected mayor and had appointed Bratton as his police commissioner. In fact the trends—like the national trends for property crime—had started much earlier as reinforced by a recent publication of BJS that shows that the rates of victimization in New York City for burglary and robbery had been dropping steadily from the early 1980s—during the period when Koch was mayor.[8] In Figure 5.1, the rate of violent crime is shown declining in the 1980s and then rising to a peak in 1990. It then drops during the Dinkins years and continues dropping in the Giuliani years. The way people talk about the drop in crime in New York City and associate it with Giuliani leaves the impression that they think that Giuliani even brought the crime rate down somehow in the four years before he was elected. It is not possible. The reductions in crime started at the end of the period when Edward Koch had been mayor from 1978 to 1989. They continued through the period that David Dinkins was mayor from 1990 to 1993 and improved further, while Giuliani was mayor from 1994 to 2001. Impressively the rates of crime have continued to trend down even if more slowly through to 2004, where Mayor Bloomberg said, "Every year, experts say we can't drive crime down any further, but happily the N.Y.P.D. proves them wrong and breaks another record." However, the basic facts do not bear out this miraculous role for the NYPD all on its own.

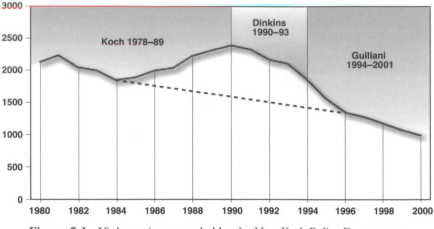

Figure 5.1. Violent crime recorded by the New York Police Department, 1980–2001.

Even so, it is possible that Giuliani made a contribution, for instance, by increasing the rate of decline and making it last longer in New York City than in other cities. His 1993 campaign focused on quality of life, crime, business, and education. His political campaign attributed his success to returning accountability to the city government. His application of strategies to hold senior officials accountable may also have contributed to reductions in the city deficit, welfare roles, and corruption. So why not crime? He invested in children, helped them to get access to health care, and increased the funds for education. He has also been associated with an extensive urban renewal program that has transformed the face of Times Square.

Giuliani claims that Compstat is the core of the success in his efforts to hold the police accountable for reducing crime. Compstat refers to the records management system for the NYPD. It was introduced in 1994 and was used to simultaneously provide information on crime recorded by police at the local, command, and city government level. Its introduction was associated with a major management overhaul of the city's seventy-six precinct commanders and top departmental management. These were heralded as knocking down the walls between traditional fiefdoms such as patrol, detective, and narcotics. It forced local commanders to be accountable for trends in crime as recorded by their officers. It was not just a data system but a process for increasing accountability. It was this—not zero tolerance or Broken Windows—that won the 1996 Innovations in Government award from the Kennedy School of Government at Harvard University.

Unfortunately, the innovations in management structure in New York City were not associated with systematic evaluations that enabled the citizens of New York City or of the world to know with any degree of precision what contributed to the significant reductions. There is no scientific evaluation of the impact of Compstat on rates of crime. However, there are three analyses of the reasons for the drop in the crime rate in New York City that I find useful to assess what contribution Compstat made. One is the work of Kelling himself who had gone on from his earlier work at the Police Foundation to become an adviser to Bratton on security on the New York transit system, and then to Bratton when Giuliani brought him to power as police commissioner in New York City in 1994.[9] The other is a book that analyzes all the data available on alternative explanations for the drop in crime rates in New York. The book was written by Karmen, a professor at John Jay College, which is a university that caters primarily to current and future police officers in New York City.[10] The third is a post hoc study by the U.S. National Crime Prevention Council done in collaboration with the International Centre for Prevention of Crime when I was still its chief executive.[11] Unfortunately, the media did not take much interest in these studies. They were happy to allow "bull to baffle brains."

Kelling was one of the authors of the speculative article titled *Broken Windows*, which the Giuliani and Bratton team used to justify their strategy of cracking down on misdemeanor offenses.[12] In fairness to Kelling, he went back to the data in the late 1990s in an effort to check out what difference those new strategies had made in New York. He did his own statistical analysis of trends in the 1989–1998 period to verify the extent to which Broken Windows had worked. In an important article for the Manhattan Institute, Kelling and a doctoral student reported on a statistical assessment of the relationship between increases in misdemeanor arrests in New York City and the reductions in rates of violent crime from 1989 to 1998.[13] This article is the principal piece of scientific evidence used by the proponents of both Compstat and Broken Windows to prove that these policing techniques worked. Kelling claimed that Broken Windows policing during 1989–1998 prevented over 60,000 violent crimes, or a 5 percent reduction. If their claim was correct, this would show the impact of Bratton efforts to get the police to use misdemeanor arrests strategically to tackle violence. While 60,000 violent crimes is an impressive statistic, 5 percent is more modest and puts their efforts in perspective—always remembering that their strategy was not only expensive in paying for police officers but also expensive because the persons arrested had to be housed and paid for in correctional institutions.

Unfortunately, their claim to have shown a causal connection between arresting more New Yorkers for misdemeanor offenses, and so this 5 percent decrease in the violent crime rate, goes beyond what co-relational analysis can prove. However, it undeniably confirms that Bratton used the Compstat process to increase misdemeanor arrests. More likely, it reflects a coincidence that Giuliani and Bratton introduced their process for Compstat and so the increases in misdemeanor offenses in the middle of the decline in violent crime.

In 1970, Zimring called attention to the conundrum of the Aunt Jane cold remedy.[14] The quacks who were selling this remedy claimed that it was guaranteed to make the cold go away within two weeks. Of course, those who bought the remedy did in fact find that their cold went away within two weeks because almost all colds go away within two weeks. The claim that increases in misdemeanor arrests may be the same in as much as the violent crime was going to go down anyhow as we saw not just for New York but for the whole of the United States in the 1990s.

Kelling equated misdemeanor arrests with the application of the Broken Windows theory. In his article, he illustrated how some NYPD officers used discretion to decide whether misdemeanors were used to stop persons urinating in public. It is impossible for me to follow the logic as to how stopping persons urinating in public would stop murders with handguns. If this 5 percent reduction really came from increasing misdemeanor arrests, then it came from the action by NYPD to stop people carrying handguns, shut down open air drug markets, and move prostitution. There is strong evidence from the prestigious reviews such as those led by the National Research Council, Sherman and his colleagues at the University of Maryland, and the work of the National Violence Research Consortium that policing that uses misdemeanor arrests to tackle an established risk factor will reduce crime.[15] So it is likely that the NYPD tactics to shake down young adult males to remove handguns and drugs would reduce violent crime.

Kelling dismissed demographic shifts or changes in use of drugs as the reasons for the decreases in violent crime, at least for the years used—1989, 1993, and 1998. He did show unemployment to have gone up, while violent crime was going down. "Unemployment" is a measure of the number of persons looking for jobs, not how many persons are actually unemployed. Likely, as the economy improved, the number of persons looking for jobs would improve as they would think that there were jobs to get. So overall, Kelling concludes that law and order produced a 5 percent reduction but he is not sure what else contributed.

Even these conclusions on a 5 percent reduction must be put in context. Kelling was the principal adviser to Giuliani and Bratton. Normally, one would look to an independent evaluator to assess whether a particular innovation had worked. Indeed the principal difficulty with the claims of Giuliani and Bratton is that they are not based on independent scientific evaluation. Medicine in the eighteenth century was full of overly optimistic claims by the inventors and hawkers of miracle solutions. Today a claim for a medical cure is put through a rigorous series of trials before the medical profession accepts that the cure works and is sure that there are no harmful side effects. Only then will the professional bodies encourage the use of the cure.

The second source is the book *New York Murder Mystery: The True Story Behind the Crime Crash of the 1990s*. This fascinating and carefully written book is by Karmen who is an experienced sociology professor who has focused his professional work on reducing victimization and helping victims. He has an international reputation for his work on preventing car theft. Even Kelling in a footnote to their analysis refers to this book "as probably the most thorough study of the issue yet."[16] While some conclusions may be debatable, Karmen's interpretations must be taken seriously by anyone wanting to get taxes used better to lower crime rates. His analysis focused predominantly on murder and car theft as recorded by the police, which are reliable indicators of the real rates of victimization as the majority of the events are reported to, and recorded by, the police.

He grouped the explanations for the drop in crime into six categories—improved policing by the NYPD, a tougher criminal justice system, the dwindling drug scene, the booming local economy, materialization of favorable demographic trends, and changing values of teenagers and young adults. He conceded that many of the firmly believed explanations contained a kernel of truth in terms of contributing to some of the reduction. This means that there were several factors, and so Giuliani or the world press could not legitimately claim that it was all due to Compstat or Broken Windows. He also stressed that the assertions that law enforcement deterred more offenders is questionable as the crimes that dropped the most were those where the clearance rate decreased. That is, the crimes dropped where the police were catching fewer offenders. By default, this agrees with the claim that the crime rate was brought down by problem-oriented policing, where the crimes that dropped were brought down by police action to tackle risk factors. For instance, when the police take guns or drugs off adults carrying guns or drugs, they make those adults less likely to kill or traffic drugs. So it is not more law and order, but more intelligent—smarter—law and order that works.

Karmen concluded that the data clearly supported four other important contributors to the drop in crime rate. The first is the number of high-school graduates who went onto college or university, not only because it qualifies these persons for the job market but also because they commit themselves to a different nonstreet culture. The second is that the higher the proportion of hardworking immigrants, the lower the crime rate as the immigrants are rarely involved in crime. The third is that discouraging drinking to excess and in public curbs violence more than other antidrug strategies. They can be discouraged through law enforcement but also through education. The fourth is the importance of creating jobs that are meaningful and reasonably remunerated which will lure some offenders away from property crime. These four are all social policies that produce less crime and victimization. So Karmen concludes that it was a little bit of smarter law and order but a lot of changes in other risk factors that cause crime that brought the crime rates down.

Karmen also draws attention to the reality that crime rates came down in a range of U.S. cities. The reductions in murder were more than 50 percent in Los Angeles, Houston, San Diego, San Antonio, Dallas, and Boston. So, the third source of insight into what caused the reduction is an interesting analysis by the National Crime Prevention Council and the International Centre for Prevention of Crime.[17] It looked at six cities where not just murder rates but violent and property crime had come down in the 1990s. Our aim was to identify lessons that could be used in the future. The cities included in the analysis were New York City as well as Boston, Fort Worth, Denver, San Diego, and Hartford.

For this analysis, police data on crimes recorded as well as details of the actions that they had taken were collected from each of the cities. The actions that they claimed had reduced crime were compared with the scientific knowledge in the Digest from the International Centre for Prevention of Crime on what had reduced crime in the past. This meant rejecting several of the actions thought by the cities to be relevant such as introduction of foot patrols and community police stations as they had not been shown to reduce crime in the past. However, it retained actions such as targeting gangs to stop them carrying guns, working with youth at risk, and focusing on programs to help victims protect themselves against burglary because they had been shown to reduce crime in controlled experiments in the past.

A focus group meeting was then organized with key officials from each of the cities to discuss the findings, which resulted in a realization that two other factors were important in the reduction of crime and victimization. The first was the importance of political will. In each of these cities that had achieved large reductions in crime that were greater than the national average, the mayor had made crime reduction a priority. The second was the importance of mobilizing several different sectors such as schools and neighborhood associations to tackle the risk factors. So the rates came down more where the strategy not only included law enforcement but also focused on social agencies to work with youth at risk and some type of action to help potential victims to take precautions. So this study concluded that some law and order worked but prevention also worked.

Collaboration and Smarter Policing—Probable Cause for Boston Drop

In a curious coincidence of history, Bratton left Boston for New York City in 1994. The person named to become the new head of the Boston Police was Paul Evans. It is Evans who most clearly was the police leader who played a role in the elimination of youth murders in a U.S. city. Yet his main technique was neither to make the Boston police tough on crime through a Compstat process like in New York nor was it to introduce community policing as in Chicago. Rather it was to take part in and form partnerships with various community groups and the local university—Harvard. I would have liked the Boston approach to have received as much attention as New York City, because in many ways it was more successful as proven by the percentage of reductions and the return of violent crime ten years later when they stopped doing what worked.

In the period from 1994 to 1996, a full spectrum of initiatives was launched to stem the wave of juvenile gang violence. The law and order strategies were very much problem-oriented. These included "Operation Ceasefire" where the information of the frontline police officer about youth, guns, and gangs was analyzed by a team in the School of Public Administration at Harvard University led by David Kennedy. The partnership enabled the police to intervene strategically to deter youth firearm violence. Its objective was to make youth believe that there would be heavy and predictable consequences for carrying handguns and violence. The police used whatever laws they could to intervene—including aggressive enforcement of liquor, traffic, and probation violations—not laws to register or control firearms directly. The approach in Boston was targeted at young men known by the police to be involved in gangs, and so many fewer innocent citizens were stopped and frisked than were in New York. A sophisticated evaluation undertaken by Kennedy[18] and others showed that even after taking into account the national drop in rates of homicide, a part of this reduction was due to the problem-solving process. Once again, it is disappointing to note that Kennedy—the architect of the program—was also one of the researchers on the evaluation.

But the Boston strategy was much more than Operation Ceasefire. It included prevention programs such as street social workers outreaching to youth in the gangs to mediate disputes and help the youth and the families access much-needed social services. They increased the services for runaways. They put in place programs to mentor and reduce school dropouts, which as we saw in Chapter 2 should reduce violence. They increased job training and mobilized local firms to create jobs. The John Hancock Mutual Life Insurance company invested in a summer program that gave youth a greater chance of completing high school and going on to college—again programs that Karmen showed would reduce violence. The churches also got involved through the Ten-Point Coalition and tried in their way to outreach to the youth.

Youth homicide fell from an average rate of forty-four per year in the period from 1991 to 1995 to fifteen in 1998, none of which involved youth under sixteen in gun violence. Okay, these are small numbers and just for youth but this is a 66 percent drop in three years! Again there is no scientific evaluation of the total package of activities—just Operation Ceasefire—but it makes sense that the results were a lot more than just smart law and order. Certainly Evans puts the reductions down to the combination of law enforcement, social agencies, and others working together to stem the tide.

In the last few years, the rates of violence in Boston have started creeping up again. While the budget for the police department has not been reduced, the funding has been cut for many of the community services that I—and Evans—claim contributed to the original elimination of youth violence. The lesson from both the original experience in Boston and the recent rise is simple. To prevent violence, you need smarter policing and services that tackle the reasons why young persons resort to violence. But you cannot limit the sustained funding just to smarter policing. You must ensure that the funding is sustained for the programs for youth at risk. There is another lesson that will become clearer in the next chapter, which is that preventive and partnership strategies cannot be left to the determination of one police leader like Evans. If Boston had in place a crime prevention planning group like Evans was able to mobilize, but on a permanent basis, then the recent rise could have been avoided.

In light of Operation Ceasefire, the U.S. Department of Justice sought to replicate the process and launched a multisite initiative called Strategic Approaches to Community Safety Initiative. The sites most successful in reducing the incidence of gun-related violence and drug trafficking were those dedicated to the strategic problem-solving process of analyzing local crime problems and implementing and evaluating problem-oriented solutions. One can only wonder how many cities would have been successful if they had gone beyond smarter policing to also use the comprehensive approach that Evans encouraged.

Community Policing Reduces Disorder Not Volume of Crime in Chicago

Chicago also claimed a reduction in crime recorded by the police in the 1990s—not proportionately as big as New York's. Chicago with a population of less than 3 million is smaller than New York with about 8 million. It also has a smaller police force with some 13,000 sworn officers (and 3,000 civilians) compared to New York with 40,000. In the 1990s, there was also a major shift in the style of policing but this was associated with a philosophy of community policing rather than Broken Windows, zero tolerance, or Compstat. This new style of policing was known as the Chicago Alternative Policing Strategy. In part, this program was about improving relations between the police and community by getting police officers to interact more with the public and take part in neighborhood meetings.

It was associated with a criminologist—Wes Skogan—a professor of urban studies at Northwestern University near Chicago. Skogan has an international reputation for his extensive work on ways to measure how much victimization there was. He had also written an influential book on how disorder in neighborhoods increases crime. So it is not surprising that the program focused on ways to reduce disorder in neighborhoods.

The Chicago Police Department started its Chicago Alternative Policing Strategy in 1993, announcing an effort to bring police, citizens, and community agencies together to prevent crime rather than just react to it. In practice, it was mostly about bringing police services closer to various minority groups in the city who were disappointed in their treatment by the police. It included assigning police officers to particular areas of the city so that they got to know local communities who to some extent would also get to know the police officer. It included community meetings where the police officers would discuss their priorities with citizens so that the police would deal with neighborhood disorder problems such as street drug sales or prostitution because these are what bring communities together around crime.

Skogan's analysis and evaluation is unclear on the extent to which the strategy contributed to a reduction in crime. In the prototype districts, he showed reductions of 50 percent or more in gangs and drugs as well as serious crimes but he does not claim the scale of reductions across the city that occurred in Boston.[19] It has also been criticized because the rates of murder never really came down. It was heralded as a community police program that would include problem-oriented policing. Unfortunately, Chicago did not use enough of this problem-oriented strategy at the city level. The rate of murders in early 2000 was three times that of New York. That is, New York with 8 million people and Chicago with less than 3 million each had the same number of murders—600.

Although there are large differences in the rates of murder, there are relatively minor differences in rates of robbery and burglary. In 2005, BJS released a comparison of the trends in victimization in the 1980s and 1990s between Chicago, Los Angeles, and New York City.[20] Instead of just using data on crime recorded by the police, it also used data from the national crime victim survey to compare trends in burglary, robbery, and aggravated assault. These data provide a very powerful comparison because they remove police discretion in recording offenses. The study confirms the trends for crime rates to have come down in all three cities in the 1990s but shows that the reductions were in fact much bigger in the 1980s than in the 1990s. It is true that New York City ends the period with a rate of burglary half that of Chicago but this trend had been there since 1984. For robberies, the reductions in New York City also occurred in the 1980s, though the differences are much smaller by 1998 between the cities. Despite the very different policing styles, the differences in rates of victimization are not dramatic. It is socioeconomic trends and not policing styles that determine the rates of victimization whatever hype mayors and police leaders can get in the media.

IN CONCLUSION

There is no clear evidence that increasing budgets even by large amounts to pay for more police makes any major difference to crime levels. Continuing the standard ways of delivering policing based on patrols, response to calls for service, and investigation is clearly unsustainable. Much greater efforts are needed to stop the waste of taxes when so much energy is lost in responses to nonurgent calls. The 311 systems that provide a phone number to call in nonurgent cases may be helpful.

The use of misdemeanor arrests guided by Compstat in New York City may have made a small difference, though in the 1990s this did not exceed 5 percent of the reduction. Leadership by a mayor when combined with a balance between problem-oriented policing, crime prevention through social development, and situational crime prevention would have improved this significantly.

The city of Boston achieved more spectacular reductions because it focused more on problem-oriented policing and crime prevention through social development. The recurrence of the problems ten years later reinforces the importance of having a permanent office for crime prevention.

The city of Chicago showed that problem-oriented policing at the neighborhood level can reduce crime but not high-volume crimes across the city such as robbery or murder. Overall, none of these cities used the potential to reduce victimization that we have seen in earlier chapters.

If there is one message from this chapter, it is that police services must reform themselves significantly by becoming much smarter, so that they tackle risk factors to solve the problems of crime. This will require them to use police data systems much more strategically for their law enforcement activities as well as planning strategies with community agencies such as services for youth.

6

Guarantee Justice and Support for Crime Victims

Unfortunately, today large numbers of persons are still victims of crime and violence. Even if politicians act swiftly on preventive policies demonstrated in this book to reduce crime and victimization, there will still be some victims of crime who will suffer loss, injury, and trauma with few remedies. Worse still, they will be ignored and their plight exacerbated by our system of law enforcement and criminal justice.

Much of what is needed to do justice to support for victims has been agreed by governments through an international human rights instrument given the long title of the U.N. Declaration on Basic Principles of Justice for Victims of Crime and Abuse of Power.[1] This Declaration was agreed with the active support of the U.S. government, including its Office for Victims of Crime in the U.S. Department of Justice. It had also been set out in the pathbreaking U.S. President's Commission on Crime Victims in 1982.[2] This commission described the U.S. system of criminal justice at that time as appallingly out of balance before making sixty-eight recommendations to remedy the situation and floating an important amendment to the U.S. Constitution. Undoubtedly, progress has been made in the intervening years but much more is needed to do justice to support victims of crime.

If there is some good news from the results of the National Crime Victim Survey, it is that most victims will be victims of property rather than violent crime.[3] That is, they will only lose property rather than be injured. This property may or may not be worth large sums of money for which they may or may not be insured. However, it is not just the monetary value that is important to victims; it is the sentimental value too. Even the least serious of thefts may involve the loss of an object that has sentimental value: a wedding ring or a photo of a deceased loved one may not have much monetary value but may have irreplaceable emotional value. Being insured may take care of the monetary value but even this may take many months. A burglary is classified by the police as a property crime but it involves a perpetrator coming into a person's home. The perpetrator may vandalize, leave threatening messages on mirrors, or rifle through personal clothes or possessions. It can result in lasting trauma that makes it difficult for the victim to sleep or go out to work.

Victims of violent crime will be injured and traumatized. They may just be bruised in a fight but they may be knifed or shot. Some will be sexually assaulted, which is calamitous enough but this may lead to pregnancy or sexually communicated diseases like AIDS. Victims of violent crime will often need to seek medical attention or go to a hospital for which they will need to pay as they do not have insurance. They may be unable to work for short periods of time or may be forever. Some will recover completely from the injury, others will not. Some will be killed.

Whether they are victims of property or violent crime, many will be traumatized—technically called *post-traumatic stress disorder* or PTSD. They may have difficulty sleeping, going out of their house, or taking part in their normal activities for many years after the victimization. For a small but important proportion, the severe and enduring trauma and physical injury will never go away—there will never be closure. Their families will suffer trauma, not only in cases of murder but also in many less heinous crimes such as burglary. PTSD is now part of the language of victimologists and is recognized in the diagnostic standards manual for doctors. Its recognition does not make it less painful or difficult.

These tragedies are exacerbated by a law-and-order industry that is obsessed with the human rights and sanctions for suspects and offenders without recognizing the human rights of, or harm done to, victims. Yes, some small progress has been made in courtrooms where victims can testify behind screens and limitations are put on defense counsel asking questions about previous sexual history in cases of sexual assault. Yes, some progress has been made in providing support to some victims, restitution from offenders, compensation from the state, and so on, but the situation leaves a lot to be desired.

CRIME IS HARMFUL TO VICTIMS, JUSTICE IS RECOGNIZING IT

If you become a victim of a crime, you need to be treated decently, caringly, and justly even if law enforcement and criminal justice systems do not give much of their time. If you are robbed walking down the street, it should be your right to expect other citizens to come to your help. If you call the police, it should be your right to expect the officer to listen to you and assist you in getting social or medical assistance, information on what he will do, and what services can support you. If you are a victim of sexual assault, it should be your right to get an officer or counselor of the same gender. It should be your right to get medical attention and counseling to recover. It should be your right to get reliable information on how to avoid being attacked again. It should be your right to be able to seek restitution from the offender and be paid before the offender pays money to the state for a fine. If you are injured and the offender cannot pay reparation, it should be your right to get compensation from the state. It should be your right to participate in the criminal court process with legal representation to protect your safety, your search for the truth, and your need for restitution. But more than anything, you want recognition of what has happened.

Unfortunately, these obvious rights are not yet a reality. In the 1970s, there was a growing awareness among victims and some professionals working with them that victims were forgotten "orphans" of the justice system. Governments such as that of the United States were undertaking regular victimization surveys that showed who victims of crime were and what impact crime had on them. The feminist movement was fighting against violence against women by getting laws changed, multiplying the number of crisis centers for victims of sexual assault, and establishing transition houses to provide a safe refuge for women who were battered by their partners. Prosecutors were setting up offices to support victims when they had to testify in court. While all these innovations were good, they are only a patchwork because they are not available everywhere or even extensively.

Also in the 1970s, victim advocates in some U.S. states got their state legislature to adopt guidelines on how victims of crime should be treated. These were called bills of rights, even though victims had no way to enforce the right. Whatever the name, the laws provided a vision for change to get victims treated fairly and with respect. In some states, there was an office for victims of crime, whose task was to implement the rights. In New York State for instance, an office that was originally established in the 1960s to give out small amounts of compensation to victims of criminal injuries had been enlarged to fund new support programs, act as an advocate to help victims get reparation and so on.

The same issues were brought up in different countries. Academics, practitioners, and policymakers had begun to meet internationally to discuss the plight of victims and what could be done. In 1979, they formed the World Society of Victimology (WSV) to advance research, services, and awareness for victims. Some national organizations had also started with similar objectives. For instance, the National Organization for Victim Assistance (NOVA) in the United States was already organizing annual conferences for practitioners, advocates, and some academics.

So in 1982, I was able to launch a global campaign to get recognition for victims, their plight, and for practical remedies. WSV and the U.S. NOVA provided the trampoline from which to launch the global campaign. WSV had members in many different countries, some of whom were policymakers in government. The first objective of the campaign was to recognize that crimes were not just violations of criminal laws but violations of people—an issue that had been forgotten and set aside by the law-and-order system. It seems obvious but even today most systems of criminal justice are systems of law enforcement rather than protection, justice, or support of victims. Yes they may say that they are prosecuting or punishing in the name of victims but in reality they are acting on behalf of the state with little regard and a lot of disregard for victims. In Canada, the prosecutor is described as a Crown attorney and that is exactly what prosecutors do—they represent the Crown not the victim.

The second objective of the campaign was to identify what were the fundamental principles of justice and support for victims. So we proposed what should be done by governments for victims. Considering that victims did not generally have access at the time to justice or support, it was surprising and encouraging how quickly governments and nongovernmental groups worldwide came to a consensus about the need to provide support, reparation, and access to justice to victims of crime. We took the campaign to countless meetings with human rights organizations and governments. Within three years, which is a remarkably short period, we had got every government in the world to adopt a resolution at the United Nations that started with their commitment that each government

> affirms the necessity of adopting national and international measures in order to secure the universal and effective recognition of, and respect for, the rights of victims of crime and of abuse of power.[4]

The resolution called for better prevention of victimization and the implementation of measures that ensure respect for four basic principles of justice for victims of crime. The principles include support and aid, restitution from the offender, compensation from the state, and access to justice. In 1985, these principles were set out in the Declaration on Basic Principles of Justice for Victims of Crime and Abuse of Power—often described as the Magna Carta for victims.[5] It recognizes the obvious but overlooked reality that victims suffer loss, injury, and trauma from crime and sets benchmarks for what governments at all levels and civil society should do in response.

NO JUSTICE WITHOUT CRIME VICTIMS

The U.N. declaration also recognizes that the problems for victims are not just at the hands of the offender. It asserts that victims often suffer additional inconvenience, costs, and trauma when assisting law enforcement and prosecutors if they report their victimization to these authorities.

It is particularly surprising that the law-and-order industry has not done more for victims because their bread and butter is dependent on victims who report victimizations to the police and testify in court for prosecutors. Sixty percent of crime recorded by law enforcement is reported by victims. Unfortunately, law enforcement and judges still consider cooperation a civic duty and rarely provide victims with basic information about the law-and-order system, or respect their private lives, or even help them feel safe. Law and order in the United States, like in Canada or England, still does not provide rights to victims to ensure that they can protect their interests in the truth, safety, restitution, or inconvenience in criminal cases, as France has done now for four decades!

Unfortunately, victims who do report to the police today, can still expect disruption, expense, and trauma as much as better support and justice. Their frustration and pain are too often left to fester. They will be lucky to get any sympathy from the system of justice—even if the individual officer or lawyer empathizes with their pain and frustration. Further, for the unfortunate few who will be used as witnesses, they will go to court at the convenience of the judge and the lawyers, not at their own. They will not be heard, they will lose income and pay their own travel and other expenses, and they will have to live with their fears for their own safety. They are unlikely to get restitution and will often hear that the judges still order fines to be paid to the state before restitution to the victim.

For all the $44 billion spent on 911 calls and public relations by police agencies, law enforcement has done little to treat victims in accordance with bills of rights—their own included—let alone international standards. So it is no coincidence that 51 percent of those who are victims of a property crime and 66 percent of those who are victims of a violent crime will not call the police. Although the exact percentage varies by type of offense, these high proportions are a serious indictment of the law-and-order industry. Yes, the proportion for auto theft or house burglaries drops to 6 percent and 27 percent, respectively, but only because victims cannot claim insurance without it.[6] For offenses such as sexual assault or wife battering, more than 80 percent of the victims will not go to the police.

This tragic ignoring of the interests of victims is particularly puzzling because the International Association of Chiefs of Police (IACP) adopted its own "Crime Victims' Bill of Rights" in 1983. I would have expected progressive police leadership to be as concerned about victims of crime as they were, even before the U.S. government enacted its legislation and the governments of the world had declared the basic principles of justice for victims of crime. This association represents more than 17,000 members from eighty-nine countries—all of whom are in leadership positions in policing across the United States and the world. Its executive director, Dan Rosenblatt, is a former elected board member of NOVA. Their affluent headquarters are located close to Washington, D.C. They have committees that work on issues such as organized crime, car theft, crime prevention, and victims of crime. When IACP adopted their bill of rights, they urged police leadership to "establish procedures and train personnel" to implement the "incontrovertible rights of all crime victims," which call on police to treat victims as "privileged clients" by ensuring that victims are

1. free from intimidation;
2. told of financial assistance and social services available and how to apply for them;
3. provided a secure area during interviews and court proceedings, and to be notified if presence in court is needed;
4. provided a quick return of stolen or other personal property when no longer needed as evidence;
5. (given) a speedy disposition of the case, and to be periodically informed of case status and final disposition; and, wherever personnel and resource capabilities allow, to be notified in felony cases whenever the perpetrator is released from custody;
6. interviewed by a female official in the case of rape and other sexual offenses, wherever personnel and resource capabilities allow.

Unfortunately, this is one of many examples of wishful thinking when it comes to support and justice for victims of crime. Did police leadership train personnel? Did police establish procedures? Some police departments did but these are the exceptions that prove the rule. Did Giuliani or Bratton make this a priority in their Compstat procedures in New York City? Did Chicago make this a part of the Chicago Alternative Policing Strategy? Did Clinton make this a part of the Community Orienting Policing Service Office? No, they did not. Even the authoritative National Research Council study of the evidence on fairness and effectiveness of policing could only manage one index entry on victims, and that is on the characteristics of victims, not on their treatment. This outrageous situation is hardly fair to victims of crime.

To find examples of police services that provide special police stations where only women work, we have to look at the innovations made in Brazil in the 1980s, which have spread to many developing countries. Women are much more likely to report sexual and physical assaults to police if they know that they will get a female responding officer and sympathetic assistance for their situation. Yet police services in the United States like in other affluent countries have not adopted this obvious solution to encouraging more women to report. As a consequence, fewer than one in five women who are victims of sexual or partner assault go to the police.

A recent summit on policing and victims, held in the United States sponsored by the U.S. Department of Justice, again made comprehensive recommendations so that victims would get a continuum of timely support and service to heal from the trauma they suffer. It repeated some of the same recommendations from the 1983 IACP set of rights but broadened them to include information and support services for victims, access to justice, and ability for victims to influence their destiny. While the recommendations make eminent sense, they were not accompanied by any concrete action to see them implemented—more words, instead of practical action.

The police are well situated to initiate crisis support to victims and should be "first in aid" to victims.[7] They are the agency most often and first contacted by victims after a crime. They are available twenty-four hours a day, seven days a week. They call ambulances and fire departments. They can separate the parties in a dispute. They may recover property, protect the victims from an aggressor, and arrest the suspect. They are able to reassure and refer the victim to appropriate services in the community.

Victims require several things from the police investigator and prosecutor: to be kept informed of the progress of the investigation and to have their property recovered as soon as the police identify it. They sometimes want to present their views at bail hearings to protect their personal safety or talk to the prosecutor before the trial. They want separate waiting rooms from accused persons.

The police could improve their support for crime victims by simple steps that have been taken in some police departments. The most obvious steps include requiring the responding officer to provide the victim with a card that identifies the key telephone numbers of such services as the local distress center, locksmiths, criminal injuries compensation, reliable advice to avoid being a victim again, and a service that could help or refer the victim to other community services. Ideally, this card would identify both the file number of the case as well as the name of the police officer. The problem is that these simple and affordable steps are not available everywhere or even part of the reforms that have been instituted in major police departments.

Much greater use could be made of modern wireless and communication technology to ensure that the individual patrol officer can inform the victim of available services by being able to check with the dispatcher while the patrol officer is with the victim. In crisis situations, the dispatcher could also patch the victim directly through to the patrol car as it responds to the victim. Special crisis units in police agencies deal with family disputes and the care and management of children. Their uniqueness comes from their ability to cope with people in crisis and link them with agencies that can provide long-term care. Police could require that property be returned to its owner on recovery; doing so may require the development of procedures for photographing or videotaping the victim with his property. Further, detectives could be required to inform victims from time to time of their actions or explain their inaction on an investigation. This can be done relatively easily by individualizing form letters.

Even though policing is largely dependent on cooperation from the victims of crime, it has been failing victims. Victims are essential to the police as research shows that it is the victim who alerts the police in more than 60 percent of offenses. It is the victim who describes the details of the crime and the suspect. It is very often the victim's cooperation that facilitates an arrest and a conviction. Further, satisfied victims can be an important source of public support for the police at budget time. The police can get more information and public support by assisting victims. If law enforcement is to become more effective, then police agencies have to give priority to responding to the needs of victims.

Of course, helping victims after they are victimized is a good thing but helping them before is also important. The Supreme Court of Canada decided in a case known by the pseudonym as Jane Doe that police were responsible for informing potential victims of certain dangers posed by offenders. In Toronto in 1986, a serial rapist was at work, who entered the apartments of white women with dark hair living alone. The existence of the rapist as well as his modus operandi of entering over the balcony was known to the police, but they did not warn women in the area. So when he attacked his fifth victim, she sued the police for not warning her and won significant damages—many years later though. To an ordinary citizen it is obvious that the police should warn potential victims. To the police their role was to catch the offender. For me this is an important case as it shows that preventing crime at least in some special instances is more important than catching offenders even to the lawyers at the pinnacle of the system of police and judges in Canada. The book that tells the story of Jane Doe makes compelling reading while describing many other ways in which a modern and professional police department mistreat women who are victims of sexual assault.[8]

DOING JUSTICE TO SUPPORT VICTIMS

Doing justice to support for victims has to be more than the work of a few dedicated pioneers. It must be universal. But the dedication of pioneers has made a significant difference. In the 1970s, a few pioneers started support services for victims of crime in both England and the United States. In Bristol, England, Nigel Whiskin, a probation officer set up the first victim support scheme—recruiting volunteers to help victims of burglary cope with the trauma. Today England and Wales has a universal system of victim support schemes, modeled after the program in Bristol.

In the United States, the Law Enforcement Assistance Administration gave seed money to get half a dozen different programs for victims and witnesses started in 1974. These included programs to help witnesses go to court and testify, projects to ensure that victims of battering would get a police officer and a social worker, centers to assist victims of sexual assault, and services to help victims who were children cope with the system. So there was a decade of innovation, experimentation, advocacy, and research, most of which came from the hearts and energies of pioneers, who were both professionals and volunteers but many of whom had been victims of crime themselves.

In the 1970s, the women's movement was drawing attention to the lack of respect for victims of rape and domestic violence shown by police, prosecutors, and judges. They were fighting for equality and fairer treatment generally but much of their battle focused on reforming antiquated laws having to do with rape and getting police to take action on violence in the home. They were setting up shelters for battered women and crisis centers for the victims of sexual assault. They were also calling attention to the way victims of crimes, especially women, were mistreated by the police and left powerless in court.

At about the same time, prosecutors who are elected in some U.S. states were getting concerned about their popularity and so began to set up offices to assist victims who were brought to the courts as witnesses. In New York City, the Vera Foundation—originally set up to release offenders on bail—launched an innovative victim assistance agency whose initial role was to help get more victims to court to testify by making their experience less frightening. This became the New York City Victim Service Agency—the world's largest. It was this agency that was ready to provide crisis support to the victims of the World Trade Center attacks.

These disparate initiatives were gathering some momentum in North America, Western Europe, and elsewhere, through both national organizations and international organizations such as the WSV. By the 1980s, England had launched a National Association of Victim Support Schemes and the U.S. pioneers had come together to form the NOVA. But it was the President's Task Force on Victims of Crime in the United States, which acted as the mobilized legislation, funding, and programs to change this system that it described as "appalling out of balance." It made sixty-eight actionable recommendations and included a draft constitutional amendment. Its proposals covered everything from crisis centers for victims of sexual assault, services for child victims, role of the clergy, and so on to the role of the victim in the criminal court.

Such progress as has been made in the United States to implement these recommendations was helped significantly by the Victims of Crime Act (VOCA) passed in 1984. This landmark legislation created the Office for Victims of Crime with an innovative funding mechanism that protected it from competing for tax allocations against the large bureaucracies in the law-and-order industry. The Office for Victims of Crime is a national responsibility center that is unique in the world and certainly an inspiring example to other countries. Its main role is to multiply the number of services and laws that provide support, compensation, and rights to victims of crime. Approximately 40 percent of its funds are used to add funds for state systems of compensation for victims with criminal injuries and another 40 percent for multiplying systems of direct support to victims. The remaining 20 percent is used for a variety of issues, including child abuse investigations, discretionary work to shift legislation, and so on, in favor of victims and an emergency fund for unexpected calamities.

The funding for the Office for Victims of Crime comes primarily from fines imposed under federal criminal law. Typically these fines are assessed on companies and other rich offenders. Some of the more exceptional cases have involved fines of $100 million or more on banks or rich stockbrokers convicted of defrauding their customers. It is also possible for individuals to bequeath funds. In its initial years, the Office for Victims of Crime had only $70 million to spend but today its annual allotment is over $500 million—of which not a cent comes from general taxes.

Even so, VOCA has achieved many things but not yet the systemic overhaul that was called for by the President's Task Force. Impressively the Office for Victims of Crime was not content to sit on its laurels. By 1998, it had published a report on the extent to which the recommendations from the President's Task Force had been implemented.[9] They noted that only a fraction of the estimated 38 million crime victims at that time receive the much-needed services such as emergency financial assistance, crisis and mental health counseling, shelter, information, and advocacy within the criminal and juvenile justice systems. They further noted that even when there is a state constitutional right, the implementation is so weak and arbitrary that many victims do not receive what is guaranteed.

Although it is disappointing to see how impervious the system of criminal justice had been to respecting the rights of victims, their report called for renewed action. The list does not seem so different from what had been recommended twenty years earlier. Hopefully their report will have some influence on the way that the Office for Victims of Crime uses its funds, but with less than 5 percent available for discretionary spending it may take some time. They called for action to enact and enforce consistent, fundamental rights for crime victims. They wanted better and comprehensive services for crime victims. They wanted to multiply promising practices. They wanted the voices of crime victims to play a central role in the nation's response to violence. My favorite is that they also wanted professionals and students to be better educated on justice and support for victims; that means that those working for the system of law and order would be taught about how to treat victims respectfully and support them. This may take time but will qualify more police officers, lawyers, judges, and citizens in knowing what needs to be done.

Still, the U.S. victim of crime will not be treated as well as their counterpart in Europe, where the universality of support services for victims is more accepted. Although the quality of service may not be as good as in the United States, at least it will be available comprehensively. Further, medical attention and hospital services are already provided free to victims of crime because they are available universally anyhow in Europe.

The time is long overdue for adequate funds to be invested across the United States to ensure that every victim has access to basic support and that every law enforcement officer and prosecutor has qualified as an expert on how victims should be treated. It is time to ensure that the bills of rights become principles of justice for which the victim has a remedy. How much would be adequate is not so clear? If we spent $100 on average for every victim to provide support and rehabilitation services, it would amount to only $2.4 billion—slightly more than 1 percent of what is spent on police, prisons, and judges today. With $2.4 billion, it would be possible to turn the tens of thousands of underpaid victim assistance workers and volunteers into professionals remunerated at a sensible level.

JUST REPARATION FOR VICTIMS

Many victims want reparation for the damage done by the perpetrator. They expect the system to help get property stolen from them returned and to get payments for other harm. So they expect the system of justice to facilitate this by ensuring that the system does not hold their stolen property longer than needed and that the offender returns it or reimburses them. In the last thirty years, innovations have occurred to interest criminal courts in awarding restitution sentences so that the offenders would be ordered to pay back some of the damage to the victim in the criminal court instead of making the victim start another legal action in a civil court. Governments have also realized that it is often difficult to get offenders to pay restitution and so have provided schemes to facilitate the payments. In the United States, restitution is a common part of a criminal sanction, and in states such as California the state works to collect the restitution and pay it to the victims. In England, criminal courts also order restitution (called compensation orders) as a penal sentence that must be paid to the victim before any fine has to be paid to the state. The court is responsible for collecting the payments.

In the Netherlands, a program called HALT reduced and prevented vandalism by juveniles by getting them to make restitution. Under the program, which was originally launched in Rotterdam in 1981, juveniles involved in vandalism are required by the police or the prosecuting authority to repair the damage and seek assistance. It has now been multiplied across sixty-five sites. Today, there is a national agency that provides coaching and technical assistance to the local projects. The resulting reductions in repeat offending were 70 percent. This illustrates how easy it is to get offenders to make restitution and how it reduces offending.

In many cases in the United States, the offender will not be able to pay full or even partial reparation. Governments across the affluent world have set up compensation programs to make payments when such reparation is not fully paid. Typically these programs have been limited to victims who have suffered a physical injury. They go back to the pioneering lobbying of Marjory Fry who was one of the first personalities to draw attention to the lack of justice for victims of crime. She was a British lay magistrate who, in the 1960s, gave speeches and wrote pamphlets about the unfairness of the systems of reparation for victims of crime. Like most advocates for victim rights after her, she was not calling for heavier penalties for offenders. Instead, she wanted victims of crime to get compensation at a level that was similar to workers who were injured on the job.

Inspired by her pamphlets, New Zealand started the first state compensation program for victims of violent crime in 1963 and England followed suit a year later. California created its program in 1965 and led other states to do the same. This was followed by some Canadian provinces and Australian states. These programs were modest for the governments to avoid paying out more money than they could afford. Even today, little is done to advertise these programs, though some jurisdictions such as England and Wales now have an extensive Web site to provide information. Today, the British Criminal Injuries Compensation Authority pays out each year $400 million, which is about 2 percent of what taxpayers spend on police, prisoners, and judges. The total is likely more than all the compensation paid to victims of crime in the United States in a country with many fewer victims of serious violence and a much smaller population. Further compensation in the United States is often made to pay medical bills that in England are already paid by the state. Two percent of the U.S. expenditures would be approximately $4 billion—proportionately not a large sum to recognize the victims of violent crime.

BJS like the national statistical agencies in other countries undertake national crime victimization surveys to measure crime, which incidentally give us accurate measures of how many victims need to be compensated and so how much a fair program would cost—a fraction of what is spent on law and order. Nevertheless, governments have been slow to inform victims of what is available or broaden the criteria so that the group of victims who have the most need receive some redress for their losses.

Unfortunately, some governments make a distinction between the amounts that are paid to victims who are murdered. So if you are murdered by someone whose whole intention was to kill you, you will not get as much in compensation as if your murderer happened to kill you as part of a terrorism act. In New York City for instance, the families of the more than 10,000 persons murdered in the last ten years would not have got even $50,000 each, while the 3,000 victims of the World Trade Center attack got more than $1 million.

RESTORATIVE JUSTICE FOR VICTIMS

There is a growing movement internationally that talks about "restorative justice." The concept is appealing. Its proponents talk about the need to help victims and offenders to work through their feelings and reach a resolution. It is expected that this will help restore the victim to the state in which she was before the crime. It talks about the crime as being not only a violation of a victim but also of the community and so the need to restore the community.

There are several different models for restorative justice. The basic elements include some kind of meeting between the victim and offender, which is organized by a professional. Some of these meetings are called victim–offender reconciliation because the main objective is to achieve a reconciliation between the victim and the offender. While others are called circle sentencing because community members sit in a circle and listen to the victim, the offender, and community members talk about what happened before deciding a sentence for the offender.

Although the rhetoric of restorative justice is appealing to victims, the practice has one major flaw. The offender has many sources of support, including legal advice from his defense lawyer paid, if necessary, by the state. Yet the victim will not have access to a lawyer paid for by the state and often will not have a professional providing any support. So if the victim and offender cannot work out an arrangement, the offender can always go back to the criminal court, but the victim cannot because he/she has no standing.

Nevertheless, one of the prestigious groups has looked at scientific trials of restorative justice processes to see if they reduce the arrest rate of the offender. In sum, these studies show that the process has reduced the chance that a violent offender will reoffend. It seems that the offender who understands the harm he has done to the victim is motivated to work out how to avoid a similar situation recurring in the future. They have also shown that victims feel much less like retaliating against the offender after going through this process than if they went through the standard criminal court process.[10]

In the country of Rwanda in Africa, one million people were hacked to death in a horrendous genocide that saw as many women and children raped and often inseminated with HIV-AIDS. The standard criminal court process was not able to handle the 100,000 perpetrators that were added to their prison system. Therefore, in the year 2000, the state enacted a law called Gaçaça that includes some of the elements of restorative justice and that brings justice back to communities. Under this law a small group of elected citizens oversees a community justice process where victims, perpetrators, and other citizens can discuss what happened, what impact it had, and what should be done. This unique process gives victims a chance to share their pain and anger with their neighbors and provides a special opportunity to arrive at some kind of collective perception of the truth. The final decisions of the Gaçaça courts are subject to appeal to the standard criminal courts but include both prison sanctions and reparation. Although instituted in a crisis, this type of procedure, at least for victims, might make more sense in the United States than the standard process where they are effectively excluded and frustrated.

HOW WILL VICTIMS GET JUSTICE—THE RIGHT TO BE HEARD

If there is one major gap in support and justice for victims of crime, it is the lack of any way of enforcing their rights. Since 1985, several governments and several U.S. states have passed laws called bills of rights for victims. These bills of rights are just "bills of goods" as they are little more than guidelines that too many police officers, lawyers, judges, and so on ignore because they are too busy on their law and order agenda and, importantly, because there is no remedy for the victim to enforce their right. In the United States as early as 1982, the President's Task Force on Victims of Crime submitted a draft for a constitutional amendment that would have provided a limited type of standing for victims in criminal courts to get some of their rights respected.

France has given victims a role in criminal proceedings now for more than forty years. It is a system little known or understood outside France. Victims have an enforceable right to standing in a French criminal court, and furthermore, they have access to legal aid to pay their lawyer if they are indigent. While the standing comes from being the civil party in criminal justice processes, they have the opportunity to defend their interests in the search for the truth, restitution, public safety, sentencing, and related issues. While the law in France is not that different from other countries in Europe, it is the provision of legal aid that changes legal rhetoric into action. As a result, French courts often have as many lawyers for the victim as for the defendant.

But this is only part of the story, the existence of this active role for the victim has led to a large number of out-of-court settlements, where the victim and the defendant agree on the reparation that will be paid by the defendant to the victim. In their law, the court can sanction these agreements by binding over the criminal case indefinitely. France has increased the number of reparation orders for young offenders from 6,000 in 1997 to 15,000 in the year 2000.

In 1982, the President's Task Force on Victims of Crime recommended the adoption of an amendment to the U.S. Constitution. By 2004, the United States was close to the first amendment to its Constitution in several decades. This would have recognized the rights for victims to be heard and have their damages repaid. We have seen that some progress has been made for victims but the pleas to provide rights have never been accompanied by any obligation on the state to provide those rights. For instance, offenders cannot be deprived of their liberty by the state without being advised and defended by a lawyer in front of an independent court. Yet obvious rights for a person victimized by crime are not guaranteed such as the right to

- reasonable protection from criminal acts;
- redress for pain, loss, and injury inflicted by crime;
- dignity, respect, and a fair deal from police, courts, and correctional authorities.

By 2004, thirty-three states had adopted various forms of constitutional amendments, and the Congress was negotiating the wording for an amendment to the U.S. Constitution. Titled the Crime Victims' Rights Amendment, it sought to provide certain permanent and fundamental rights for crime victims. This amendment included protections for restitution, to be present and heard, and to be treated with respect. It was weak on protecting the safety of victims, though it referred to their not being subjected to decisions that disregard their safety. The operative paragraph states:

> Victims of violent crimes shall have the rights to timely notice of any release, escape, and public proceeding involving the crime; not to be excluded from such proceedings; to be heard at release, plea, sentencing, commutation, and pardon proceedings; and not to be subjected to undue delay, or to decisions that disregard their safety or their just claims to restitution; nor shall these rights be restricted, except when, and to the degree that, compelling necessity dictates.

If this clause was added to the Constitution, it would have given victims and others the right to go up to the Supreme Court to get the rights enforced. The amendment required a two-thirds majority of each of the Senate and the House of Representatives. To become law, it then required to be approved by three quarters of the state legislatures. However, it did not get that far, even when they added the qualifier that the protection of these rights will not "abridge the rights of those accused or convicted of victimizing them." But despite this modifier that left perpetrators with a veto over some rights rather than some balance between the rights of victims and of offenders, this amendment was not adopted by the U.S. Congress—a very sad day for victims of crime in the United States. It is also sad for victims in other countries who often look to the United States for leadership.

In its place, another law was adopted that provides some hope for the future as it provides funding for lawyers to work for victims to get some action on some of these same issues.[11] This law specified that a crime victim has the following rights that can be enforced by those lawyers and other provisions in the act:

1. The right to be reasonably protected from the accused.
2. The right to reasonable, accurate, and timely notice of any public court proceeding, or any parole proceeding, involving the crime or of any release or escape of the accused.
3. The right not to be excluded from any such public court proceeding, unless the court, after receiving clear and convincing evidence, determines that testimony by the victim would be materially altered if the victim heard other testimony at that proceeding.
4. The right to be reasonably heard at any public proceeding in the district court involving release, plea, sentencing, or any parole proceeding.

5. The reasonable right to confer with the attorney for the government in the case.
6. The right to full and timely restitution as provided in law.
7. The right to proceedings free from unreasonable delay.
8. The right to be treated with fairness and with respect for the victim's dignity and privacy.

The European Union in the meantime had made some progress by adopting in March 2001 what is called a "framework decision" on the standing of victims in criminal proceedings. A framework decision is a fancy title for requiring all present and future European Union governments to provide to victims of crime services, information, restitution, mediation, and even some standing in a criminal court to defend their interests.

There are fifteen operative and four administrative articles. These provide considerable precision and detail. The provisions include that the dignity, rights, and interests of victims in criminal proceedings must be recognized, so that they have a real and appropriate role in proceedings. Victims as witnesses and parties to proceedings have a right to receive information, including on services, legal advice, outcome of complaints, and release of dangerous defendants. Victims have a right to protection for their safety and privacy. They must be able to testify by any appropriate means compatible with basic legal principles. They must not be subject to undue pressure or secondary victimization. Victims have a right to restitution (called compensation) from the offender in the course of criminal proceedings, unless provision is made for a different manner. Measures must be implemented to encourage offenders to pay restitution ordered. Specialist services and victim support organizations must be available either through state agencies or the funding of non-government organizations. Police officers and lawyers must be trained to be in contact with victims, particularly those who are vulnerable (Article 14). Victims resident in another member state must be able to make a complaint from their state of residence. States must cooperate to ensure the effective protection of victims' interests (Articles 11 and 12).

Unlike the bills of rights in the United States, the European Union provides a modest remedy to push the governments to implement these provisions. So governments must report on what they have done, and the European Union can pay for independent evaluations as to whether victims are indeed receiving the services that were promised.

France is transforming justice from a sterile retributive process to a living form of justice between victims and offenders internationally. That country influenced the statute that establishes the International Criminal Court, which creates a permanent court to convict persons who commit such abuses of power as genocide, crimes against humanity, and war crimes.[12] The statute does not limit the role of victims to that of a witness. It enacts provisions to provide support, protection, reparation, and participation to victims that go further than previous international courts and creates by example a standard for national jurisdictions. Special projects are examining how to establish both the victim witness unit and ensure the representation and participation of victims. The statute contains many provisions familiar to lawyers in North America but it calls for the court to establish principles relating to "reparations to, or in respect of, victims, including restitution, compensation and rehabilitation." It allows for the use of trust funds, which can receive fines and forfeitures. Victims may make representations to the pretrial chamber of the court. They may protect their interests by presenting additional evidence even if the accused pleads guilty.

At the trial stage, victims are provided with the opportunity to protect their personal interests with wording borrowed from section 6 (b) of the U.N. Declaration:

> Where the personal interests of the victims are affected, the Court shall permit their views and concerns to be presented and considered at stages of the proceedings determined to be appropriate by the Court and in a manner which is not prejudicial to or inconsistent with the rights of the accused and a fair and impartial trial.

Such views and concerns may be presented by the legal representatives of the victims where the court considers it appropriate, in accordance with the Rules of Procedure and Evidence. A unit will be established in addition to the victim witness unit to ensure the representation and participation of victims in the process.

To realize the principle accepted for so long in France and now also adopted in Germany nationally as well as by a growing group of governments internationally, it might cost $1000 per victim going to court. If only a million of the 24 million victims of crime have their case go to court each year, this would require $1 billion a year—about half a percentage of what is spent on law and order.

IN CONCLUSION

There is much rhetoric on doing justice to support for victims. The actionable recommendations are well established but not yet acted on. Police must pay more attention to victims of crime or risk losing their source of information for most crime. This must include making female officers available to female victims, referral of victims to community support services, and providing information on how to prevent repeat victimization.

Much needs to be done to make support services universal, to get restitution paid, and to provide equitable compensation. Some restorative justice processes that involve the victim reduce the desire for retaliation and so are important ways of preventing crime. Systems such as Gaçaça provide more comprehensive models for restorative justice than the patchwork of processes in place today in the United States.

But what is needed more than anything else is to provide victims with a remedy to get that action, likely through a constitutional amendment such as that almost adopted in 2004. While the United States has not endorsed the International Criminal Court, the statute of Rome provides the single best model of how victims should be dealt with in a court system.

Although the estimates on costs are only ballpark figures, doing justice to support for victims would require an allocation or reallocation of 4 percent of what is currently spent on law and order—2 percent for support and legal remedies and another 2 percent for reparation. If one percent goes currently to victim assistance and compensation, this is only a reallocation of 3 percent. Why not?

7

Make Cities Tough on Causes

When you are asked where you live, you respond by giving the name of a city or by saying that you live near such and such a city. Much of our identity is tied up with cities. When we think about solving problems such as garbage or public transit, we think about the city. But when we think about dealing with the crime problem, we think about the police department. This perception must change if we are going to prevent crime and victimization.

City management and governance are the keys to preventing crime in a way that is affordable and can be sustained. While it may seem strange to think of your mayor and his or her administration as the heroes in fighting crime, it is in fact their planning and oversight that will solve the crime problem. It is they—not the police department—who are the key to getting agencies able to tackle the risk factors that cause crime. Hollywood and the local press may not make heroes of them yet.

This may seem counterintuitive to you and indeed to your Mayor but who else will mobilize school boards, housing services, social services, sports programs, neighborhoods, citizens, and even business activities to tackle the risk factors that predispose kids, families, neighborhoods, schools, and whole cities to crime. They are the ones who can improve access to programs to assist with early childhood upbringing, provide funds to recruit and train mentors for teenagers at risk, multiply youth centers, increase investment in education and training for excluded youth, and so on. They can ensure that parking is designed to reduce theft and casual surveillance improved on streets to reduce victimization. They can encourage local leaders who strengthen neighborhoods. They can insist that the police department become more problem oriented and get the police and agencies such as schools and social services to work together to deal with problems such as school dropouts. They can ensure that there are local services to support victims and foster peaceful resolution of conflicts.

My plea for cities to get tough on the causes of crime is not the first time that advocates for better quality of life have argued that cities hold the keys to prevention. Toward the end of the nineteenth century, prestigious commissions concluded that the massive numbers of death from epidemics of cholera, typhoid, and dysentery—all water-borne diseases—could be prevented by cleaning up the rivers. So municipalities began to clean up our sources of drinking water and so put an end to these killers. It was local government not doctors that defeated disease in a sustained and affordable manner.

The same is true for crime. It is cities more than police or lawyers or corrections that will solve the crime problem. Cities must clean up their investment in social programs to eliminate many of the immediate causes of child abuse, wife battering, violence by youth, and so on. Yes, police must be a partner in that process because they can enforce laws that reduce some of the risk factors, and they can share their maps of crime with agencies like schools that can make a significant difference to rates of crime.

Cities also collect and control a part of the taxes that we pay. Cities want to keep their residents. So they want both safer neighborhoods and cities where taxes do not spiral out of control. They want cities where taxpayers stay so that there is a sound tax base. In fact cities are the most important bulwark against this cycle of more crime, more police, more taxes, and more crime and yet more police and even more taxes.

Leaving crime to police may make police officers into heroes who deserve higher pay because their job is sometimes dangerous and require more staff because there is more crime. But police services operating in the standard way are unable to address most of the risk factors that cause violence; so rates of crime go up or down despite what we pay to them. Further when crime goes up—or experience it is going up because of media coverage of a sensational and exceptional incident—more police will be hired and so we will have to pay more.

Cities that take on urban safety with a plan and a preventive perspective will be able to avoid increases in taxes that over time lose sight of what is cost-effective and sustainable. Cities must do this on a permanent basis and not just in reaction to a wave of youth violence. Yes, cities need help from other levels of government to plan well and do what works but they are the unit of government closest to the problems and solutions, and so they are the most able bodies to focus actions where they are needed. They must target more investment in services that will tackle the risk factors that cause crime.

U.S. MAYORS CALL FOR CITIES TO BE TOUGH ON CAUSES

The United States Conference of Mayors (USCM) is the national organization that brings together the mayors of the major cities in the United States. In 1932 when 14 million people were unemployed in the United States, USCM was launched to get the federal government to fund cities to solve this national problem. In the 1980s, it was focused on the growing problems of violence and drugs in U.S. cities. In an interesting partnership between the USCM and their Canadian and European counterparts, they organized two major conferences. These conferences clarified the importance of the role that cities must play to prevent and curb crime and drugs by implementing tough measures on the risk factors that cause crime. The USCM with their two partners developed two action statements. The first was called the agenda for safer cities, which was followed by the second declaration on ways to implement that agenda.[1] These provide the clear vision for cities to be tough on risk factors that cause victimization and so reduce crime in an effective and sustainable way.

The USCM partnership with European and Canadian mayors was brought about by a realization that more law and order in the 1980s had not been enough to stem the tide of rising violence and drug abuse. It was also influenced by the visionary leadership of Gilbert Bonnemaison who had become the champion for cities to be tough on causes of crime in France. He was the Mayor of a suburb of Paris and an important national politician in France. He had grown up in a difficult suburb of Paris where he saw firsthand how family breakdown, school failure, prejudice, and poverty led to crime and conflict with police and then time behind bars. In 1982, he became the president of a task force of mayors in France who took the bull by the horns in finding solutions to urban crime. The mayors and their constituents had lost faith in the ability of the French police and legal system to solve the problems of crime in their communities. So their task force traveled across France to discuss with local politicians and ordinary citizens what needed to be done. The report from this task force became the corner stone for getting local politicians to be tough on the risk factors that cause crime. Their report became known as the Bonnemaison Report and is quoted in legislative committees in Australia, New Zealand, Canada, and so on.

The Bonnemaison Report emphasized the need to balance a modernized system of enforcement and criminal justice, with being smarter about tackling the factors that put people and neighborhoods at risk to crime. It agreed that crime would be reduced if the government did more through general policies to reduce inequalities of income, employment race, and gender. But importantly it identified the unique role that cities must play in using local policies to target the risk factors that cause crime—the key to success. Its insistence on "secondary" crime prevention—tackling risk factors—would later be supported by all the prestigious commissions that have been mentioned in this book. Yes, we need to improve national policies on jobs, education, and social services. Also, we need to modernize law enforcement. But more than anything, we must target the situations that put youth and families at risk to crime—regardless of what those national policies do. In this case cities have a unique contribution to make because they can organize more cooperation between agencies dealing with youth and families to tackle the risk factors locally.

It is common to hear those on the political right, dismissing investment in more education or housing as not being effective to reduce crime. It is just as common to hear those on the political left say that heavier penalties will not reduce violence. Bonnemaison stuck to truth and good sense, not political hyperbole. He asserted that it is not just a question of spending more taxes on education or policing, but a question of being smarter in getting agencies to work together more effectively and target their efforts on the situations that are at risk.

Shortly after the report was published, disadvantaged and immigrant youth were involved in riots that took place in several French cities—similar to the riots in 1991 and again in 2005. The French media headlined incidents of vandalism and rodeos in a suburb of Lyons, the second largest city in France. The photographs of disadvantaged and immigrant teenagers racing and burning stolen cars on city streets were sufficient for the new government to start implementing the recommendations of the Bonnemaison Report. The French government created a national crime prevention council (NCPC) to mobilize ministries such as education, social services, policing, and justice to work together to tackle the causes by implementing the Bonnemaison Report. It was a clear statement that crime would not be reduced just through police and justice measures. Rather the path to success must be based on local government tackling local risk factors.

Unfortunately, the French government did not invest the funds that were needed, even though the structure made good sense. In fairness, they did not have access to the prestigious commissions that we have now. Also they had not lived the repetition and expansion of those riots that occurred in 1991 and more dramatically in 2005. However, we can learn from those commissions and from the failures by the French government to invest in services for youth at risk.

Even so, the French NCPC had assisted eight municipalities to establish committees to organize municipal crime prevention strategies. These committees brought together city councilors, police leadership, school principals, and others to look at the local crime problems and work out how they could tackle the risk factors that caused the crimes. The plans were to be based on a diagnosis of the local problems in order to jointly tackle situations leading to crime. This diagnosis was to include an analysis of the quantity, location, and nature of crime, an inventory of the action of the various agencies at the local level, and a proposal for new initiatives in the next few years. These plans were discussed in open meetings so that the citizens had access to what was being decided. In the 1980s, more and more of these local municipal councils developed. Even though there was not adequate investment of funds, they were able to achieve some success and even show that crime rate was coming down in these pioneering cities compared to neighboring cities with similar problems.

Before the process could be spread consistently across France, there was an election that brought a new central government. This did not kill the strategy outright but it did slow the trickle of funds. So in 1988, Bonnemaison turned to North America to get recognition that he thought would persuade the new government to invest more. He wanted me to help him do this. Together, we orchestrated the two major international conferences in Montreal and then Paris, which not only endorsed his approach but also developed a clear vision on the role that cities must play to reduce crime.

First, we went to the Federation of Canadian Municipalities, which is the voice for local government across Canada. Then we started meetings with the USCM who were suspicious of the contribution that we could make to their problems from outside the United States, but they knew that they were struggling to find solutions to their escalating rates of murders, violence, and drug abuse. So the USCM joined with their Canadian and European counterparts to organize the first North American European Conference on Urban Safety and Crime Prevention in Montreal in 1989. Mayors came from all over the United States, Canada, and Europe to the meeting. Initial views varied from Mayor Koch's extreme law and order approach—not so dissimilar from Giuliani's—to views about social prevention from the mayor of Strasbourg in France.

After four days of meetings, the U.S. mayors joined their European and Canadian counterparts in announcing their commitment to implement an agenda for safer cities, which called on cities to play a new but key role in reducing crime.[2] Their vision called for a response that goes beyond police, courts, and corrections to prevent crime by bringing together housing, social services, recreation, schools, police, and justice to tackle the situations that breed crime. It called for elected officials at all levels to exert leadership. It listed causes that seem obvious from earlier chapters but are overlooked by the current law and order approach in the United States, including

- poverty, unemployment, lack of affordable, decent housing, and an unresponsive education system;
- a growing underclass created by blocked opportunities;
- the disintegration of communities and families, exacerbated by inadequate parenting;
- difficulty for individuals to connect with the community;
- drug abuse, in part caused by other factors mentioned, and drug trafficking.

It identified what should be done about these problems. I find it fascinating to see how many of their proposals based on good sense were consistent with the recommendations from the prestigious commissions that were to be published ten or fifteen years later, and based on the accumulation of research in the years after those conferences. The mixture of policymakers, practitioners, and law enforcement at these conferences was very much ahead of their time. Again this list of actions seems obvious but the $200 billion of taxpayers' money spent on law and order does not address these issues. Here are some of the key recommendations on how to prevent crime:

- There should be early investment in children, pre- and postnatal care, and nutrition assistance for mothers and children.
- Youth should be involved in the development of crime prevention policies, particularly those relating to health, recreation, training, and employment.
- Employers must provide fulfilling work opportunities, particularly for dropouts.
- Municipal and other orders of government must tackle family violence, sexual assaults, and abuse of women and children.
- Police, judges, social workers, doctors, and teachers should be trained in interagency settings to promote interagency prevention.

It called for crime prevention strategies to be tailored to local urban needs but not limited to the resources of cities. Again these seem obvious. Its recommendations on prevention include the following:

- Local efforts must be supported by national policies that provide stable, direct, and timely funding and allow for local flexibility in program design for prevention.
- National strategies to prevent crime must go beyond support for the police, including addressing poverty and unemployment.
- International efforts must provide local officials with successful models for prevention and expertise.

It also called for international efforts to control firearms and drug trafficking. In sum, it called for police, courts, and corrections—*law*—to continue but to be joined by practical prevention—*more order*—based on the individual and collective actions of social agencies such as schools, housing, and social services.

Following this, the USCM continued its partnership with their Canadian and European counterparts to organize the second International Conference on Urban Safety, Drugs and Crime Prevention in Paris in 1991. This time groups such as the International Association of Chiefs of Police were visibly on the program as were the U.S. NCPC. This very high-profile conference again produced a declaration that drew attention to the problems of crime and victimization, including crime against women.

The declaration included the following statements:

- Municipalities are strategically based to bring together those who can change the conditions that generate crime, but other levels of government must provide financial and technical support.
- Comprehensive crime prevention must give priority to partnerships that find better solutions to problems of child poverty, youth, schooling, housing, policing, and justice.
- Crime prevention must involve long-term action that is responsive to short-term needs.

It also reaffirmed that

- effective models for action are available from governments that have national crime prevention structures, from cities that have established municipal crime prevention structures, and from individual projects that have reduced various types of criminal activity;
- governments are unlikely to reduce national levels of crime until they spend substantially more on prevention; current spending for prevention is inadequate in all represented countries.

CITIES MUST SUSTAIN ACTION ON CAUSES

But the declaration did not stop there. One specific sentence called for all increases in police, courts, and corrections to be matched by investments in prevention. The USCM with its partners committed to four actions to get effective crime prevention delivered which are as relevant today as they were then.

1. Governments were to invest in "domestic security" by doing more to meet the needs of young persons at risk and alienated groups.
2. Governments were to establish national crime prevention centers to improve national policies, undertake research and development, and foster implementation of prevention by cities.
3. Municipalities were to mobilize the leadership from housing, schooling, youth families, social services, police, and so on to be tough on causes.
4. Governments and cities were to ensure that the public participates in these comprehensive crime prevention efforts and understands their relevance.

The USCM had participated actively in these events and committed itself to fighting for and doing what it had agreed. But the common sense of investing in prevention—along those lines again to be confirmed by numerous prestigious commissions—is hard to bring about. It requires political leadership and vision. The willingness of cities to take charge must be supported by other orders of government who can provide the resources and skills. This did not happen.

Unfortunately, the Clinton administration did not invest in what the USCM wanted at that time—what prestigious commissions would show to be effective and capable of being sustained! Instead they continued what the prestigious commissions were to show would misspend taxpayers' funds. They wasted the opportunity by spending on prison construction and more police so that even more billions of dollars were tied up in *more law*—not more prevention—*not more order*. Further, these increased expenditures followed the start of the significant decrease in rates of violent crime.

Some cities in the United States did attempt some efforts at prevention along the lines proposed by the USCM. But they did not commit the funds to the planning and implementation of prevention, which were and are needed. In 1992, seven Texas mayors got together to form MUSCLE—Mayors United on Safety, Crime and Law Enforcement. This included the mayors of Arlington, Austin, Corpus Christi, Dallas, Fort Worth, Houston, and San Antonio. MUSCLE went to see Governor Richards of Texas to ask her for much tougher penalties against crime, including extending the use of the death penalty already widely used in Texas. Governor Richards sent the mayors home with a promise that she would look at the penalties, once they had addressed the local causes of their crime and drug problems.

MUSCLE turned to the U.S. NCPC—perhaps best known for their mascot McGruff who wants to take a bite out of crime. NCPC had just come from the two international conferences where they had exchanged ideas with mayors and officials from cities that had organized to be tough on causes. NCPC took up the challenge to work with the mayors, the police departments, and citizen groups. Despite the hundreds of millions of dollars that each of these cities was spending on police, courts, and corrections, NCPC went in with little more than hope. They established a grassroots partnership in each of the cities, which brought together folk from the police, city hall, and various citizen coalitions. They assigned personnel without any experience because that experience did not exist in the United States.

Most of the cities did develop a plan to reduce crime, violence, and drug abuse but without the significant reallocation or investment of resources called for. Even so, there were results. Fort Worth moved from being the most violent city in the United States to a more average city by cutting its violent crime rate by a bigger percentage than New York City. San Antonio established the first Crime Prevention Commission in the United States and is now the second safest large city in the United States. Others made more modest gains. Of course, these initiatives coincided with the nation-wide reductions in crime and violence and so may have occurred despite the work by NCPC. Given the total lack of external resources in terms of funds and lack of training and experience, it is a miracle that they achieved anything.

These efforts led to another grassroots-based program of the NCPC called Comprehensive Community Strategies. It was supposed to build on the success from the Texas cities. In practice, it helped identify some grassroots leaders who were making miracles happen with little assistance from government. Undoubtedly, these leaders deserved medals for their bravery, commitment, and skill. But why leave community initiatives at prevention to volunteer efforts and courage when millions and indeed billions of dollars are being poured into the law and order side.

In 2001, the NCPC started to use similar techniques to encourage six U.S. states to embed crime prevention in state policy and practice. Within five years, they wanted to launch self-sustaining movements in those states to make prevention the policy of choice for reducing crime and violence. The goal makes so much sense, given what we have seen from the prestigious commissions in this book. However, the method to bring about the change was totally inadequate for the challenge—they also needed a miracle. They invited a group of persons working on crime prevention from Arizona, California, Connecticut, Iowa, Kentucky, and Oregon to form a statewide network in each state. The networks shared ideals about prevention and looked at steps that could be taken. They met nationally from time to time. They recognized the difficulties of bringing about changes in bureaucracies but did not come up with the funds or the legislation.

In an environment where such significant funds and resources are being used to support the system of law enforcement and criminal justice, one can pray for miracles but cannot expect voluntary initiatives to make a significant difference. These fell far short of the vision endorsed by the USCM just a few years earlier, which called for substantial increases in spending on prevention. More than anything, it called for strong political leadership and courage. It insisted that local efforts must be supported by national policies that provide stable, direct, and timely funding. In Texas the mayors were supportive but not investing significant funds. In the six states, the governors needed to provide leadership and funds, which they have not yet.

There have been other attempts to tackle the risk factors that cause crime at the community level. They also depend more on hope than sound funding. These include both the Weed and Seed initiative and Communities that Care. Strikingly absent from the support of these efforts is the permanency of city government backing this drive—identified as essential by USCM. However, evaluations of some of them show that crime rates went down during the years that they were active. Unfortunately, these evaluations are hard to interpret once again because crime rates went down everywhere in the United States in the 1990s when the programs were running.

Over and above the unfortunate name, Weed and Seed is an initiative of the U.S. Department of Justice launched in 1991. It was planned to provide a combination of being tough on criminals—law enforcement and prosecutors weeding out violent criminals and drug traffickers—and tough on causes—public and nongovernmental agencies seeding better human services to prevent, intervene, and restore communities. On paper, it has some merit as it is a comprehensive multiagency approach to crime prevention, community revitalization, and law enforcement.

There are many limitations to Weed and Seed as a program likely to have a significant impact on the reduction of crime and victimization in the United States. For instance, there is no requirement that the activities initiated be based on blueprints or other proven practices or on the recommendations from the prestigious commissions. They do not follow a systematic way of identifying where their activities should be focused. But undoubtedly, the biggest limitation is the level of funding. The evaluators for the National Institute of Justice concluded that the program was more successful when the funds were more concentrated.[3] As the funds did not exceed $750,000 a year, it is not surprising that they could not make a large difference unless the area was small.

Another program that has been promoted in the United States, England, The Netherlands, and Australia is called Communities that Care. It is designed to tackle the risk factors that predispose youth to persistent delinquency. It is based on sound research about how childhood and youth experiences predispose young persons to persistent delinquency and other social difficulties. It has focused particularly on stopping drug abuse by improving services to young children and their families. Some of the services such as PATHS follow the Blue Print models discussed in Chapter 2. PATHS stands for "promoting alternative thinking strategies" and is a program to help children in elementary school learn to manage better their emotional and social life. The effect of the program is to reduce behaviors by the children that are believed to lead to later delinquency and drug abuse. I have been unable to find an overall evaluation of how many communities are using it or its impact. As it has recently been taken over by the Substance Abuse and Mental Health Services Administration, we may be able to learn about its potential in the next few years. However, once again it is not supported yet by significant funds or the type of sustainability that would come from citywide endorsement.

CITIES DIAGNOSE CAUSES AND PLAN SOLUTIONS

Although U.S. cities have not invested in a major way yet in these or the Bonnemaison approach, some other countries have taken it more seriously. The most notable of these is England and Wales, where the Blair government adopted the Crime and Disorder Act in 1998, which requires every local government to form its own community safety and crime prevention partnership, jointly chaired by the police chief and the mayor. More than 350 local governments and associated police services have established a community safety partnership. These partnerships have each produced a community safety plan for the period 1998–2001 as well as 2001–2004 and now 2004–2007, based on an audit of the crime problems with the participation of police, social services, health, education, and many other agencies, and the public. It also must identify targets for reductions in victimization and evaluate whether the results are achieved. The analysis or audit of the crime problem in their city is the basis for a three-year plan to reduce crime and victimization in the city.

The British strategies evolved from a variety of sources including their own prestigious commission—the Morgan Report in 1991—on the role of local government in crime prevention. They were also based on learning from other countries, research and evaluation, and listening to what the public wanted. They were prepared in part by political analysts, the Audit Commission, Her Majesty's Inspectorate of Constabulary, and leading government researchers. Although I am sure that no British civil servant would ever admit this—even if they realized it—the local government partnerships were the application of the Bonnemaison strategy to every community in England.

There were some differences in the way that the process is used between England and France with respect to the chair of the partnership was to be held jointly between the leaders of city council and the police force, and for reasons difficult to follow the legislation did not require schools to be an obligatory part of the process. However, the British were clever enough in the legislation to require that the partnership analyze the extent and causes of the crime problem in their city through an "audit" and then develop a three-year strategic plan to tackle the crime problem. These analyses and plans are available to local citizens and over the Internet.

In 2004, Birmingham's use of this approach won that city the European Crime Prevention Award. Birmingham is the second largest city in England and Wales with a population of about 1 million—slightly smaller than Dallas. The city was successful in reducing crime significantly in eight high-crime and deprived neighborhoods. Its community safety partnership undertook an analysis of the crime problems in these eight areas, and then acted to solve the problems. The program reduced youth crime by 17 percent or two and half times more than comparable areas. The investment of $1.4 million achieved savings of $140 million—a stitch in time is as good as nine. The community safety partnership partnered with the renowned British consultancy and advisory group—Crime Concern—to pull off this success. Crime Concern helped the coordinator of the program to know what to do and to establish strong partnerships between agencies able to tackle the causes. While 17 percent may not sound large, this is the contribution of the process to the reduction. That is, it should be compared with the much smaller but proven 5 percent that the Giuliani process got in New York City—albeit for a much larger city.

These British programs have many sensible characteristics that follow-on from what the USCM wanted to see. They are run by cities with support from other levels of government. They address risk factors such as early childhood, youth, and family experiences. They focus on job training and creation. They include law enforcement but go beyond it to address social risk factors.

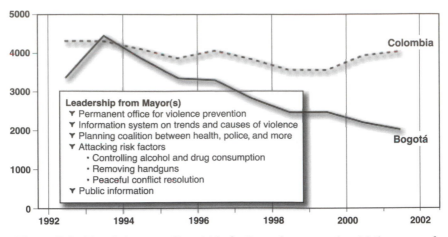

Figure 7.1. Trends in rates of homicide for Bogotá, compared to 13.5 percent of national rate, 1992–2001.

It may seem strange to say that cities in North America can learn from Latin America but the city of Bogotá, Colombia, presents an inspiring example of how a city can reduce violence by tackling the risk factors that cause violence. Bogotá has a population of 8.5 million, which is marginally bigger than that of New York City. Today its crime rate of thirty murders per 100,000 population is below the crime rate of thirty-six for Washington, D.C. The importance of Bogotá to less law, more order is that it illustrates the dramatic reductions that can be achieved through the leadership of the mayor, or in this case three mayors.[4]

As shown in Figure 7.1, in 1993, there were 4,452 murders in Bogotá but this had been brought down to 1,993 in 2001. Unlike the United States, the national rate of homicides in Colombia only decreased by 10 percent between 1992 and 2002. So the large reductions in the murder rate were not an accident. It was the result of deliberate actions of its mayors and was based on science rather than speculation. Bogotá did exactly what the USCM had called for in 1991. Starting in 1995, each successive mayor that served a three-year term or less continued a deliberate action to reduce violence in the city. The mayors included Paul Bromberg, Enrique Peñalosa, and Antanas Mockus. Its mayors established a city crime prevention planning office called an observatory—a secretariat to analyze the causes of violent crime and propose solutions—better investments. This office undertook epidemiological analyses of the distribution of violence across the city and the risk factors that were associated with murder.

Everyone asks me well what did they do. My answer is that I have already told you. They did it by setting up a permanent office for violence prevention that established an information system on trends and causes of violence. This office orchestrated a coalition between police, health, and so on to plan ways to tackle the risk factors causing violence. On the basis of the data, this office recommended ways to better control alcohol and drug consumption, remove handguns, and assist victims to find nonviolent ways to avoid their feelings for retaliation. Importantly, the mayors listened to the recommendations and acted on them. So they implemented deliberate interventions such as removing handguns—achieved in part by the police—forcing a curfew to keep men off the streets—achieved in part by the police—and helping victims of violence and insults to avoid retaliation.

No, neither the mayors nor the national goverment misspent taxpayers' money on more police, prisoners, and judges, nor did they pass harsher criminal penalties hoping for deterrence that does not work and so locking up an increasing number of offenders. They did not just add more police, pay for a visit by Giuliani, or introduce Compstat. The most important ingredient to their success was that they organized to solve the problem by identifying and tackling the risk factors that cause violence. The reductions in crime are spectacular and undoubtedly were brought about more by deliberate policy than the reductions in U.S. cities, which just coincided with drops in violent crime rates. While the evaluation is not there to prove it for Bogotá or the U.S. cities, the reductions followed logical interventions targeted to the causes.

OFFICE TO PREVENT CRIME TO FOCUS CITIES ON RISK FACTORS

Cities are still facing unacceptable levels of street crime. They are facing unacceptable levels of child abuse and violence against women, particularly behind closed doors. They are facing problems of bullying and violence in schools. These are unacceptable.

For some cities, the crime rates are not getting worse. For others, gunfights and street violence are surging back. Whether the rates of violence will climb rapidly or slowly as the economic cycle turns down, cities need to plan now how to keep rates of victimization down and drive them lower. The root of rising crime is precisely the lack of sustained investment in prevention and good planning. Victimization is too important to be left to calls to 911, who dispatch a police officer to respond. Good business may be built by taking care of one client at a time. Yes, police who take care of one victim at a time will build business for policing. But what we want is not a growing police business but a deliberate lowering of rates of violence and property crime. Less victimization will be achieved affordably and in a sustainable manner through the leadership of local government not policing, lawyers, judges, or prisons. We have seen the actions that were demanded by the USCM. We have seen the lack of investment in crime prevention through social development in various small initiatives in the United States. We have seen the insistence by Blair through legislation in England and Wales that every city engages in a

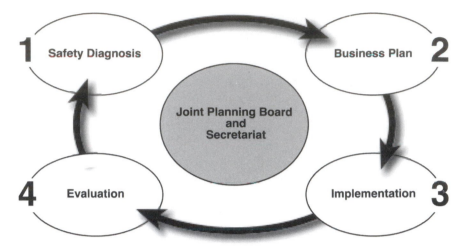

Figure 7.2. City crime prevention planning office.

planning process to prevent crime. We have seen some success in England and the example of Bogotá.

If we are going to make a difference to violence, then we have to learn from these experiences and be much more strategic. We must focus on the risk factors that cause violence. We have to balance the expenditures on law and order with funds invested to sustain the social programs that will make a difference. A smarter city will establish a crime prevention planning office, which will support a permanent and ongoing planning process and increase the investment in programs for youth at risk, to outlaw violence, to improve ways to watch over property, and to get a smarter police service.

The International Centre for Prevention of Crime in its Digest in 1999 looked at the recommendations from mayors, the analysis of experts, and the practical proposals developed by agencies such as NCPC in the United States and Crime Concern in England and Wales.[5] There is a consensus from these groups that the way to reduce crime and violence in cities is affordable, child and women friendly ways is to create a permanent planning process that coordinates the energies of the agencies such as schools, housing, and police to tackle the risk factors that cause crime.

The key to this process is a permanent city crime prevention planning office. The process is logical. Figure 7.2 shows the generic parts of the process. In simple terms, there must be a permanent planning board with staff that manages a process of diagnosing what are the main crime problems facing the city. Because victimization is caused by a series of different risk factors, it is important to assemble on the board the key agencies that can influence those factors.

Among those risk factors are problems of school failure and dropouts. It is in schools that bullying takes place. Schools also bring together youth at the ages when they are most likely to be involved in crime. So the top officials who manage schools should be members of the board. Also among the factors are problems of families in crisis who are unable to provide consistent and caring upbringing to youth. Violence in the family must be addressed. And therefore services that work with families must be included. In many cities there are services that work with youth to help them get job training and find themselves. So these services must be included. Recreation and sports are other important issues, and so they must be at the table. Often it will be important to include representatives from particular ethnic or neighborhood groups where crime is a particular problem. The police are important members of the board because they have computerized information about the crimes reported to them but also because they have an overview of crime in the city and the factors associated with it. They can also enforce legislation that tackles risk factors such as excessive alcohol or illegal handguns.

Successful programs that tackle risk factors and cause victimization will require an investment in diagnosing the problem. So the first step is to analyze the problem in collaboration with the agencies that can solve the problem. They will need to implement and monitor the solutions—probably bringing in consultants and trainers to assist the services to implement the plan.

They must look to proven solutions, not seductive political hype and media myths. Many prestigious commissions have reviewed all the evaluations of what works and what does not. Just look at the list again—organizations that have earned trust on other issues: The World Health Organization, the U.S. Surgeon General, the British Audit Commission, the International Centre for Prevention of Crime, the National Research Council, the U.S. Department of Justice, the British Inspectorate of Police, and so on. Cities can put this knowledge to work to reduce crime and victimization.

The advent of computerized mapping technology enables officials in different parts of the city bureaucracy to see the same picture—the geographic distribution of crimes recorded by the police. From Santiago in Chile to Birmingham in England—not just Compstat in New York City—police services have the capability to produce these maps. Unfortunately, their potential is not used as the crime analysis unit of the police service does not have a way of showing the maps to the agencies that can use them strategically to tackle the causes of crime. These maps confirm how the rates of offending and victimization are concentrated and related to other factors such as poverty, broken families, lack of sports facilities, and so on. So the agencies working with broken families or sports facilities need to see them and put their services to work to tackle the problems.

Because so many of the crimes that occur behind closed doors such as child abuse and violence against women do not come to the attention of the police, it is important for cities to use other means to make these evident to planners. Data from child protection agencies, for instance, give some indication of child abuse. These can be supplemented by surveys in schools that measure bullying and violence at home. Surveys of women may help indicate the extent of violence against them. Focus groups can supplement these systematic data.

Cities must also look at the priorities for their taxpayers. They must consider whether an investment now in tackling the situations that put youth, families, and neighborhoods at risk to crime and victimization can justify an investment in changing those risk factors. Lack of action now means taxpayers will pay later for increased policing. Preventing crime before it happens is cost-efficient and also cost-beneficial, as healthy kids and youth make productive adults later on. For example, to reduce serious crime by 10 percent, you can either provide incentives for at-risk youth to complete high school—which also contributes to enrolment in postsecondary education—or spend over seven times more in tax dollars per household to increase incarceration. Safe communities provide for a better quality of life, and enhanced opportunities for economic development, investment, and tourism. Just as cities have plans for transportation, the environment, and public health, so they must have a public safety plan that sets priorities on how our taxes should be used to reform police services and invest in prevention that tackles the risk factors that cause crime.

IN CONCLUSION

Mayors of U.S. cities agreed on the importance of going beyond law enforcement to engage the agencies such as schools and social services to tackle the risk factors that cause victimization. They also agreed that cities must be able to sustain the planning and implementation to tackle those risk factors. They wanted support from other levels of government to make this happen.

Unfortunately, other levels of government put their money just into increasing law enforcement without investing in crime diagnosis and planning. Efforts to tackle causes by cities in the United States have been based more on hope and short-term projects than sustained and adequately funded diagnosis and solutions.

Examples from England and elsewhere show that cities can bring crime rates down further and be prepared for resurgence in crime as the national economic and demographic forces reverse. They need offices for crime prevention at the city level to get agencies and citizens to tackle the risk factors.

8

Shift from "Pay for Law" to "Invest in Order"

I wrote this book to show how truth and good sense could be used to prevent victimization by investing in youth and families without continuing to squander hard-earned taxpayers' money on expensive and reactive law enforcement and criminal justice. I have reviewed the truths on crime prevention achieved by prestigious commissions comprising of many different professions—auditors, public health doctors, criminologists, and police chiefs. From these truths and good sense, I have identified a comprehensive range of actionable recommendations that would help reduce crime, support victims, and provide a better way to invest our taxes than they are being used today. I have insisted that cities must take the lead in coordinating the different public sector groups such as schools, social services, and law enforcement agencies to tackle the risk factors that cause crime.

ACTIONS TO PREVENT CRIME BASED ON TRUTH

I call for a major shift in public policy by all orders of government. This shift must take us from our overreliance on reactive law and order. Whatever the talk, our taxes today are used primarily to respond to crime by being reactive, reactionary, and repressive. We pay for professional law enforcement officers, professional lawyers, professional judges but the gains in terms of reducing victimization are not significant. We are misusing our taxes on expensive, comparatively ineffective, and short-term solutions. We also pay to incarcerate far too many young adults, particularly of racial minorities. We waste taxes on a system that is tough on victims of crime, tough on taxpayers, and tough to use to get crime down.

In contrast, *Less Law, More Order* has shown many better—preemptive and preventive—ways to reduce crime by investing in better futures and that are much less burdensome to taxpayers. The most important ones are described in the following sections.

Invest in Youth in the Community

Investing the resources in services to provide more mentors, programs to avoid dropping out of school, assistance to go to college, job training, employment, and so on, we can keep many more at-risk youth in the community away from crime. We can reduce bullying and violence in schools by programs that address the root causes of bullying. We can establish centers for youth to catch up on homework and spend time with adults who provide role models for their positive development. We can prevent crime significantly without affecting much the taxpayers by investing in public health nurses to work with mothers who lack the capacity on their own to provide consistent parenting to their children. These programs can be most successful if we combine them and focus them in communities that are most at risk.

Stop Violence against Women and Children

Violence against women can be prevented by continuing to improve the access of women to income and child support as well as family law that enables them to choose whether to stay in violent relationships. Giving women access to counselors and police who are female will encourage more to say no to violence. Reductions in spousal violence will avoid the exposure of children to witnessing or suffering violence so that they are less likely to grow up to be violent. Teaching peaceful conflict resolution and how to avoid destructive decisions to youth will prevent violence.

Help Neighbors Watch and Design to Reduce Crime

We can watch out for our persons and property by collaborating better with our immediate neighbors and using judiciously our new electronic gadgets— closed circuit television, alarms, mobile phones, and computer technology. We must foster local neighborhoods where the residents collaborate. We need to design houses, cars, and other goods to reduce the ease with which they lead to crime. We must not use universal protections such as airport security or car immobilizers, without tackling the social risk factors that push persons to commit the offenses in the first place.

Tackle Risk Factors with Both Prevention and Enforcement

In our efforts to reduce crime, success will not only come from prevention but an intelligent combination of prevention and enforcement, which is targeted to risk factors such as illegal handguns, destructive driving, alcohol, and illicit drugs, will help to a larger extent. We can reduce crime by getting our police to be smarter with their resources and becoming more problem oriented, for example using data more strategically and in partnership with schools and other agencies to tackle risk factors. The model encouraged by Evans in Boston is particularly important, though aspects of Compstat in New York City that help focus policing on risk factors will also provide payoffs.

Do Justice to Support Victims

Being treated with respect and dignity is a human right for the victims of crime. It should be protected like any other right by a legal remedy. We must ensure that victims are treated respectfully by police who are first in aid, by support services that make a difference, by courts that order and enforce fair restitution, and by constitutions that guarantee participation and representation to victims even in a criminal court. These must be universal not just a patchwork. We must invest in processes that help victims understand what happened and get the truth.

SHIFTING REQUIRES SKILL, INDEPENDENCE, AND PLANNED CHANGE

How do we go from shifting our overreliance on law and order today to smarter enforcement and more prevention—less law, more order—for tomorrow? While we are investing in prevention, what do we do about the seemingly insatiable needs of 911 calls, crime, and victimization today? How do we succeed in helping our political elite go from being followers and "misspenders" on law and reaction to being leaders who invest in order and prevention—making the reforms now in our cities, schools, police, and so on? How can long-term success be achieved when elections take place every four or five years? How can we help them shift funds to new programs that have been shown to be successful from traditional programs that are not?

Commission after commission confirms that in order to tackle the risk factors that cause crime a strategy through a combination of prevention and enforcement works much better than the standard reactive responses that dominate today. I have advised ministers across the world on this knowledge and the international guidelines. I have worked inside government and also watched from the outside, as progressive politicians struggled with bureaucracies for small successes. I helped found and run the International Centre for Prevention of Crime affiliated with the United Nations. Unfortunately, many politicians, their advisors, and their bureaucracies are influenced by exaggerations of how crime was reduced in New York City and a belief that public outrage will be assuaged by more police and harsher penalties.

Our politicians do not need to stand by helpless, while the bureaucracies maintain what does not work and our mass media and schools neglect to disseminate what does. It may seem like a tough assignment to shift from a system that has grown bigger and bigger over the last quarter century, where two million people earn their annual salaries directly from law enforcement and criminal justice in the United States alone. It is equally tough to get cities to take on a new role when so many other services depend on their good governance. It will be difficult to persuade schools to devote some of the time from writing, reading, and arithmetic to educate youth in conflict resolution and good parenting.

Fortunately, there are already good examples of how law and order has been reformed, which demonstrate that it is possible to make such changes. The biggest of these was started by the Safe Streets Act in the United States in 1968. Unfortunately, this did more to increase the size and expenditures on law and order than investing on truth and good sense, but it shows what legislation and funds can do. In 1968, the world's biggest and most extensive program was launched to shift law and order from the doldrums to a professional system of law enforcement and criminal justice to cope with the challenge of crime in a free society. This program was created by the 1968 Safe Streets Act which started the Law Enforcement Assistance Administration (LEAA). For fourteen years, it pumped billions of federal dollars into the modernization of the law-and-order industry as well as research and development on prevention and justice for victims. Some preventive projects were encouraged such as the community crime prevention program in Seattle that was discussed in Chapter 4. Although the majority of the energy and resources went in to law and order, the model of passing a federal law to create an office to champion reform with significant funds to support change is a good one. It just needs to be used to invest in implementing the recommendations from all the prestigious commissions rather than misspending on what does not reduce crime responsibly.

The British government showed in part how to use truth and good sense to prevent crime in 1998 with their Crime and Disorder Act. They are reforming the youth criminal justice system in England and Wales through the independent Youth Justice Board (YJB). I particularly like their use of persons with knowledge of the recommendations from the prestigious commissions to key roles. For instance, the first chair of the YJB was Norman Warner who previously had been the political adviser to Tony Blair on crime prevention and community safety and then the adviser to the British Home Secretary, who was responsible for drafting the Crime and Disorder Act. So he was able to bring his substantive knowledge and political skills to help the board to succeed. The members of his board were brought together from experts in the key areas, such as policing, criminology, and resettlement of offenders. They also appointed the lead author of *Misspent Youth*, Mark Perfect, as the first chief executive officer. It was this report produced by the Audit Commission that recommended a radical shift in how the problems of youth crime were to be managed in the United Kingdom. Using these experts in key roles makes successful implementation much more likely and is a major reason for their impressive achievements.

The YJB also was organized to "plan change." By this I mean that it invested in training the persons who would implement its strategies and set standards as to how those strategies would be implemented. Successful innovation requires persons who have the skills to manage change and the skills to implement the programs. They must be supported by mentors or consultants that can help them weather that process. The end result is a series of proven successes such as significant reduction in delays between arrest and trial for young offenders in England and Wales as well as demonstrated prevention of youth offending so that only fewer young persons are arrested.

Another impressive example is the Office for Victims of Crime (OVC) in the U.S. Department of Justice, which was created in 1984. Following her legendary work as the chair of the U.S. President's Task Force on Victims of Crime, Lois Haight Herrington was appointed the first chief executive officer of the OVC and so got it launched in a way that generated impressive momentum for change in favor of better support and compensation for victims of crime. This office planned the shift by funding training of the persons who wanted to make innovations that would support victims better. Initially they were helped by the U.S. National Organization for Victim Assistance, whose executive director Marlene Young had developed training courses for all the major professionals who work with victims of crime. The result is that every state has a crime compensation program, services in support of victims have been multiplied, many states have adopted constitutional amendments, and so on. The OVC report on implementation of the Presidential Commission on Victims of Crime shows significant progress, even if more remains to be done.[1] Once again the appointment of the main author of the task force to the operational post led to the impressive achievements.

All three of these programs have a degree of independence from the standard police, courts, and corrections system as well as significant if the funding is too little. All three have had an impact nationwide. The LEAA and the YJB are using revenue from general taxes. VOCA is using fines on rich offenders and has created a large constituency of services and programs that are dependent on their funding. I am sure that the success of all three depended on the knowledge and experience of the top officials, the independence of the board itself, and their accountability for success.

A different approach is for the public to force legislators and judges to implement recommendations from prestigious commissions. In 2000,

61 percent of California voters adopted Proposition 36 that forced judges and legislators to invest $120 million in a proven treatment program for nonviolent drug users in the community. Heralded as smarter policy, the proponents had brought to the attention of the voters facts such as the effectiveness of the community treatment that had been shown to reduce criminal activity by 72 percent, expected annual savings of $100 million, and so on. Proposition 36 included a provision for evaluation of the implementation to demonstrate whether it was achieving its goals. It is particularly interesting to note that once voters are given facts, they vote in line with recommendations consistent with truths. Interestingly the evaluations have confirmed the original research, and so Governor Schwarzenegger is planning to renew the funds for Proposition 36, demonstrating both the success of the program and the force of public pressure.

MADD provides another inspiring success story. It has succeeded in getting a shift from inaction to extensive legislative change and awareness of fatalities and injuries from driving. It lobbied successfully for the presidential task force to look at what should be done about traffic fatalities. Armed with these conclusions, it holds government accountable for making a difference to the number of road fatalities and implementing measures that MADD believes will work. The victim movement in the United States other than MADD has not yet focused on issues of prevention enough but they could take a leaf out of MADD's book to get a presidential task force to recommend ways to sustain the reduction in violence at affordable cost to taxpayers.

CRIME BILL FOR OFFICE FOR CRIME PREVENTION

In 2002, the United States and other governments accepted at the United Nations sophisticated Guidelines for the Prevention of Crime that are consistent with much of the conclusions from the prestigious commissions. These place an emphasis on the role of planning at the national, state, and local level, draw attention to the importance of multisectoral strategies for tackling the multiple risk factors that cause crime, and make recommendations for training, data, and ways to empower governments at all levels.

Inspired by the success of OVC and the British YJB as well as these guidelines and the experience from advising ministers on how to make the shift, I am calling for governments to put in place an Office for Crime Prevention at the most senior level. The main objective of this office is to implement the recommendations from the prestigious commissions. It must have the same permanency and independence that was the key to the success of VOCA, the YJB, and indeed LEAA. This is the vehicle to spearhead the planning and partnerships that must mobilize law enforcement, justice, education, sports, training, and social services section around a joint process of diagnosis, planning, implementation, and evaluation to tackle the factors that foster crime.

This must foster a change in the culture of police, justice, education, and other agencies that make public safety one of the ultimate objectives for which they are accountable.

The office must also influence primary social policies such as investment in schools, job creation, job training, preschool programs, public health nurses, controls over handguns, measures to make cars and roads safer, and so on. These primary social policies are in place for their own reasons rather than to prevent crime. So the board can only draw politicians' attention to some of the additional advantages in terms of crime reduction.

Such offices are likely to be most successful, when they are established at the most senior level of government. The head of the crime reduction responsibility center should be at the same level as the head of departments responsible for policing or corrections or parole. Comprehensive crime prevention strategies—led and organized by the Office for Crime Prevention at each level of government—will lead to a quality of life where crime rates have been reduced significantly below international norms without any unwarranted increase in taxes and with a better use of present social and criminal justice policy dollars. It must deliver the following five actions.

National and Statewide Plans to Shift from Reaction to Prevention

It must provide a vision and business plan for significant reductions in crime and violence. It should cover a ten-year period and be as ambitious as reducing crimes such as burglaries, robberies, car thefts, and so on by 50 percent below what would have been expected from general social trends while avoiding increases in the proportion of taxes spent on crime control.

The British government has set clear targets over time for the reduction of burglaries and car theft, which were initiated before their reelection in 2001 and are being pursued now. In England, these were specified over a period of years, so that the bureaucracies have time to reorganize the focus area. While Compstat may not have achieved all that it claimed, the general mission for crime reduction was clearly enunciated, and then the commanders were held accountable for bringing the crime rates down. The bureaucracies must be accountable for reducing victimization even further as measured by the national crime victimization survey.

To achieve these goals, governments need to develop a national business plan for local government, police and justice services, school boards, and others to tackle the social, situational, and area risk factors that cause crime. The business plan would identify benchmarks to be achieved over those ten years, like MADD holds governments accountable for reductions in traffic fatalities. In federal jurisdictions where the responsibility for tackling common crime is divided such as in the United States or Canada, the plan would need to be determined jointly between the federal and other orders of government.

Another part of the vision should be to deliberately increase the investment in strategies that tackle risk factors that cause crime. This would include programs to help kids at risk to complete school, be mentored, and use centers for recreation and homework. It should highlight how investments in prevention will save loss and suffering. So if governments acted to halve the rate of common crime, they would be able to prevent many citizens from suffering the loss, injury, or trauma each year. In addition, they would be able to reduce the need for private security and improve civic vitality. This would have helped reduce the need for handguns for self-protection. Further, they could reduce the costs of incarceration, if they chose to reduce its use consistent with reductions in crime and violence.

Shift 10 Percent from Law and Order to Organize for Prevention and Victim Support

It is important to get a permanent agency such as those set up in Scandinavian countries, Australian states, Belgium, Canada, and France. Unless the agency has access to permanent and significant funds like LEAA, VOCA, or the YJB it cannot fulfill its mission.

My solution is to recommend that the equivalent of 5 percent of enforcement and criminal justice dollars be allocated to crime prevention that targets key risk factors, 3 percent to victim support and justice, and 2 percent to the training and data systems that are needed to sustain the shift. By making it a fixed percentage, the funding is independent and assured. It is difficult for a small new agency such as an Office for Crime Prevention to argue successfully for funding, whereas large bureaucracies such as police or corrections services are well organized to protect and expand their budgets.

As I have shown in earlier chapters, investing 5 percent on prevention planning and reform would reduce crime significantly and sustainable at least in high-risk areas by 50 percent or more. I have persuaded Canadian parliamentary committees to endorse this rule that 5 percent of all expenditures on law enforcement and criminal justice should be allocated annually to planning and prevention activities that would not otherwise have existed. The argument is that every agency can afford a 1 percent reduction. So each year 1 percent is taken so that it increases the budget slowly and does not threaten the budget from which it is taken. The 1 percent must be protected from the crises that inevitably occur and for which politicians will take any funds not spent. If the amount is increased by 1 percent each year, within five years 5 percent of what is spent on law and order will be used for the reform process that is needed. It is doubtful how much can be achieved with only 5 percent. These funds are over and above the funds spent by the different sectors such as education, social services, or policing that might be devoted to prevention-type activities.

The same step-by-step approach must be used to provide the funding for victim assistance, support, and justice. So that total for both prevention and victims will reach 10 percent of what is currently being spent—likely $20 billion.

Support Local Government Leadership to Deliver Crime Prevention

Less Law, More Order has shown how the leaders of our cities—not our police chiefs—are in the best position to organize for crime reduction. Just as cities have plans for transportation, the environment, and public health, so they must have a public safety plan that sets priorities on how our taxes should be used. This involves the mayor establishing an office to develop an investment plan to reduce crime and victimization, with a protected budget that ensures that the plan is implemented and the results are achieved. A smarter city will know where its different crime problems are located and what can be done to tackle the causes of those concentrations of offenders and victims. A smarter city will stop spending more and more each year on police and set tighter priorities on responding to calls for service. It will steadily and determinedly reduce the need for those calls by investing in programs for youth at risk, to outlaw violence, to improve ways to watch over property, and to get a smarter police service.

Develop and Train Crime Prevention Professionals

It is not easy to go from a fundamentally reactive system of police, courts, and corrections to one where you are focusing on prevention. The inertia in doing things the same old way is enormous. Although some of what is called for in *Less Law, More Order* can be achieved by investing in more public health nurses and doctors. One of the barriers to successful prevention is the lack of trained and skilled personnel to implement the new activities. So schools, colleges, and universities need to develop programs for persons to become professionals in crime prevention. Advanced graduate degrees will develop executives and innovators. Professional associations need to be launched to set standards. It is important to provide opportunities for those working in the present system to retrain so that they can pursue their professional careers within the new paradigm. It is vital to develop the skills that are needed before large investments are made.

The efforts to provide this training and education are still weak. The central theme in earlier chapters is that successful prevention flows from some type of analysis of the problem to identify how one can eliminate the risk factors that cause victimization. The analysis must lead to a plan and priorities and so to action and ultimately evaluation to see if there have been changes in crime. While this problem-solving strategy seems simple, its application requires considerable sophistication, particularly where it involves the coordination of work from different agencies such as schools and police services who are not used to cooperating at institutional level in their planning.

In the United States, the National Crime Prevention Institute at the University of Louisville provides a range of courses that focus on ways to protect potential victims. University of Rutgers provides material on situational crime prevention. In England, a number of universities have developed courses that include crime prevention and community safety but these are not organized to support the certification of crime prevention professionals. One of the most interesting exceptions to this rule is a distance learning course at the University of West of England in Bristol. Ultimately what is needed are courses and standards on how to do problem analysis that identifies how to tackle social factors that predispose young persons to crime. It must deal with how cities and other orders of government can plan to reduce crime. A new Institute for the Prevention of Crime at the University of Ottawa is interested in filling this gap for Canada, the United States, and elsewhere.

We also need to create careers within institutions that are committed to using these new talents. So changes will be needed in police services, school boards, municipal government, and so on. Shifting from law and order, to less law, more order is like shifting from an exclusive reliance on doctors and hospitals to public health strategies. There is a need to work with the senior executives to help them shift their organizations to include a preventive planning capacity.

Crime Concern is a unique organization set up in England to help cities, local communities, and even neighborhoods establish effective ways to reduce crime and increase feelings of safety. It is like a football coach to football players. It provides the advice and support to help cities, youth agencies, police, community groups, and local residents to get effective crime reduction activities going. It was Crime Concern that helped the city of Birmingham to win the European Crime Prevention Prize for its citywide reductions in crime, as mentioned in Chapter 6. Crime Concern also runs some programs itself such as the Youth Inclusion Programs that have been so successful in reducing youth crime, as discussed in Chapter 2. There is a need to develop such an organization in the United States and Canada.

Establish Data on Risk Factors, Victimization, and Location

A clear signal that the government is serious about the reduction of crime is for its leader to articulate targets for crime reduction and hold the bureaucracy accountable for results. For this to work, the governments must have access to independent indicators of crime levels such as victimization surveys that are not influenced by police reporting practices. Many countries have reduced the government deficit by setting targets. Yet they have failed to apply the same approach to crime.

Although the police statistics can be helpful for prevention, there are many better indicators. Their performance must be assessed in terms of the reductions in the number of victims, measured by victimization surveys, or the numbers of fatalities, measured by the number of persons admitted to hospital emergency rooms with injuries from interpersonal violence or car crashes. A national crime victimization survey provides trend data on whether the crimes covered are going up or down over time. It provides a framework for comparison of local data. It also offers a possibility of evaluation of outcomes. It identifies the extent to which repeat victimization is taking place. As discussed in Chapter 1, the United States has undertaken a national crime survey to measure rates of victimization every year since 1973. A local survey needs to be developed for use by cities so that progress can be monitored at the city level. Second, cities have to start using them in their policy and funding decisions.

National surveys on the development of offending provide a basis to assess persistent offending and identify general factors that predispose young persons to become offenders. These surveys provide critical data to inform national social policies. They can also be used to evaluate how innovations in policy have affected the likelihood of young persons becoming persistent offenders. The evaluation of the Perry Preschool discussed in Chapter 2 used such a long-term follow-up to demonstrate its remarkable long-term effectiveness and the impressive social and financial dividends from the investment.

IN CONCLUSION

Less Law, More Order has demonstrated the wealth of strategies that prevent crime. I have grouped these under five headings:

1. Investing to keep at-risk youth in the community away from crime
2. Stopping violence against women and children
3. Helping prevent crime by getting neighbors to work together and better industrial design
4. Tackling risk factors with both prevention and enforcement
5. Doing justice to support for victims.

Given the wealth of truth and good sense on preventing crime, which is not being used, we need to make a shift to much greater investment in these strategies, which will help reduce victimization, slow down and reverse the increases in taxes for reaction to crime, and reduce the number of persons incarcerated. I recommend that we achieve this through a comprehensive crime bill that creates an Office for Crime Prevention to

1. develop national and state plans,
2. reapply 10 percent of funds from law and order to organize for prevention and victim support,
3. ensure that cities establish problem-oriented crime prevention plans,
4. develop and train crime prevention professionals, and
5. establish data systems on risk factors, victimization, and location of crime.

9

Conclusion: Bust Causes, Not Budgets

Less Law, More Order concludes that crime prevention will significantly reduce the victimization of Americans for much less cost to taxpayers than the expansive and expensive reactive policies of the last thirty years. It has made actionable recommendations based on the scientific and sensible conclusions from prestigious commissions in the United States and internationally. These recommendations call for greater investment in social development, public health, and law enforcement strategies that tackle the risk factors that cause crime. They also call for greater effort to meet the needs of victims and provide them with enforceable rights.

There are two common objections to making these investments. The first objection is that the political elite believe that the public does not want prevention, they only want more punishment. Yes, some voters want more punishment. But wanting more punishment does not equal wanting less prevention. These are two separate issues. In fact, the public is strongly in favor of prevention. For at least fifteen years, Americans have consistently been two for one in favor of investing in education and job training rather than spending on more police, prisons, and judges to lower crime.[1] Figure 9.1 adapted from Gallup Poll shows an unmistakable trend.

The second objection is that it would cost too much to invest in effective prevention and a decrease in law and order would lose too many jobs in policing and enforcement. So I am proposing key elements for a Crime Reduction Bill—based on truth and good sense—that shows how small reallocations of public funds can achieve large percentage reductions in crime and

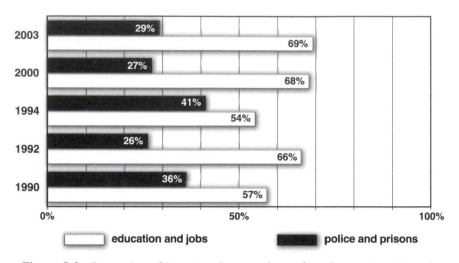

Figure 9.1. Proportion of Americans by year who prefer to lower crime through additional money and effort in education and jobs rather than police and prisons.

victimization. This bill proposes retraining and reorganizing law enforcement agencies—rather than layoffs—as the key to more effective and smarter law enforcement.

My proposal assumes that the federal government has been transferring $5 billion to the state and local governments. Instead of inciting more police, prisoners, and judges—more taxes—it call for greater investment in programs that prevent crime, and hence less taxes. In the first year, it proposes that the federal funds would be used to assist the state and local governments to reallocate just 2 percent from the ineffective and costly enforcement into prevention that works. Each year an additional 2 percent would be added until 10 percent has been reallocated in the fifth year. Figure 9.2 shows how these proposed budget reallocations would be used. Based on an estimated $200 billion spent on law enforcement, prisoners, and judges, it shows the total amount in billions for all the state and local governments.

The evidence in *Less Law, More Order* is clear that these funds will bring about significant reductions in victimization, while improving the quality of life for disadvantaged children, youth, women, and neighborhoods. The first five line items are programs that flow from the recommendations of the prestigious commissions discussed in *Less Law, More Order*. Here are some estimates of the percentage reductions that are possible, remembering that it is the accumulation of reductions from using the comprehensive set of proposals that will assure the real gains.

The line item on youth and gang programs includes efforts to foster mentoring, school completion, youth centers, job training, and so on for youth at risk. Individually, these have been shown to produce reductions in

Prevention Programs	Budget in billions	% of total expenditures
1.1 Youth and gang crime	$2	
1.2 Violence against women and children	$2	
1.3 Violence relating to cars, guns and substance abuse	$2	
1.4 Neighborhood disorder and burglaries	$2	
1.5 Crime enabled by industrial and environmental design	$2	
Subtotal	**$10**	**5.0%**
Victim support and justice		
2.1 Support services	$2	
2.2 Reparation to victims	$3	
2.3 Realization of rights	$1	
Subtotal	**$6**	**3.0%**
Ways to sustain prevention and victim support		
3.1 City wide community safety planning	$1	
3.2 Making policing oriented to risk factors and victims	$1	
3.3 Training of prevention and support professionals	$1	
3.4 Local victimization and crime data bases	$1	
Subtotal	**$4**	**2.0%**
TOTAL	**$20**	**10.0%**

Figure 9.2. Proposed budget allocations in billions of dollars for a Crime Bill to lower victimization and taxes.

victimization from 15 to over 50 percent. So a combination of these programs should produce at least a 25 percent reduction in national rates of crime and possibly much more within a three- to five-year period.

The line item for programs that prevent violence against women and children includes improved employment and child support arrangements for disadvantaged women. These would build on many important initiatives already in place. Such programs would lower violence against women by 20 percent or possibly much more over a three- to five-year period and have a ripple effect on violence against children into the next generation.

The line item for programs that prevent violence associated with cars, guns, and substance abuse implements a range of proven programs nationally. These would foster less destructive use of cars—even less dangerous and drunken driving—while building on many achievements to reduce road fatalities and injuries. They would promote peaceful resolution of conflicts and tackle the risk factors that lead to substance abuse. These should achieve a 20–30 percent reduction in violence over a five-year period.

The programs that reduce neighborhood disorder such as those discussed by the Chicago Police Department reduced violence and other offenses by nearly 50 percent. Programs that reduced residential burglaries such as those proven in England and Wales produce reductions close to 70 percent. So the combination should achieve large reductions—say 50 percent—in both property and disorder offenses.

The fifth line item proposes programs that will lower crime by making crime prevention a requirement for approval of industrial and environmental design, and so lowering the potential for easy profits from crime and increasing the risk of offending and effort to commit a successful crime. The exact percentage reductions are less clear, though some of the examples used in this book— steering wheel locks for instance—have all but eliminated the victimizations in the past. This requires a continuing effort as the offender is quick to find a way around the successful design. Nevertheless, large percentage reductions should be achieved.

The comprehensive implementation of a combination of all these programs will result in much more than the reductions from using just one line item and so could reach a solid 50 percent reduction within ten years if other things stayed equal. This will also result in a multiplier effect. As Americans gain confidence in their personal safety, they will need to buy less private security services and devices. They will also have less need to carry handguns for their self-protection, which will reduce further the fatalities and injuries from handguns. Overall, these should reduce the homicide rate in the United States to the much lower levels found in Canada and Europe.

Nevertheless, these will not eliminate victimization as it is known today. So the group of line items on victim support and justice will still be more than necessary. Each line item follows recommendations from Chapter 6 and builds on the important achievements by the Office for Victims of Crime and their partners in the state and local governments. The item for support services would enable community and law enforcement to establish more comprehensive services for all victims. The item on reparation for victims of crime would bring the United States closer to the amounts paid to victims of crime in England and Wales and reduce the disparity between victims of terrorism and common crime. The item on realization of rights for victims— the right to standing and participation—would move victims of crime closer to the situation in France where victims are regularly represented in criminal courts by a lawyer so that they can recover restitution, protect their personal safety, get closer to the truth, and get justice.

Both the prevention programs and the funds for victim support will require some infrastructure and new skills. These are proposed in the group entitled ways to sustain prevention and victim support. The first item will enable state and local governments to establish offices for crime prevention as proposed in *Less Law, More Order*. In the law enforcement sector, there are already some initiatives to foster more problem-oriented policing, such as the Community Oriented Policing Service of the U.S. Department of Justice. What is proposed here are more funds and ambition to help law enforcement agencies—not just individual officers—comprehensively adopt a problem-oriented perspective and work closely with other agencies such as school boards and public health to tackle the risk factors that cause crime. It also calls for the training and standards so that police can be first to aid victims as foreseen by the IACP incontrovertible bill of rights for victims more than thirty years ago and reemphasized by the IACP recently.

The line item for training of prevention and support professionals focuses on new education and standards for many of those working in law enforcement, public health, youth services, victim services and municipal government, and so on. For prevention and victim support to be successful, they must have new skills and should meet explicit standards. The item for local victimization and crime databases would enable municipalities to combine their different police, social, health, and school datasets for planning purposes as well as undertake local victimization surveys.

But this is not just about preventing victimization but also about saving taxpayers' dollars. Within five years, the states and local government should save much more than the $20 billion reallocated because they do not need to spend more on police, prisons, and judges at this time as they can use the extra capacity garnered in the last decade. Actually they could save this $20 billion and more now because the crime rates have already gone down. Further, the program proposed here is going to achieve much greater reductions in victimization if socioeconomic trends stay positive as well as slow down increases in victimization, if the socioeconomic factors that brought crime down turned negative.

There are many different formulae for bringing about savings in law and order expenditures by the state and local governments. The most obvious influence from the federal government would be to tie their transfer of funds to a business plan requiring a reduction in law and order expenditures sufficient to save the funds provided federally within five years. At first sight these figures seem unachievable but a reduction of 10 percent in taxes spent on police, prisoners, and judges in five years is much less than the 25–50 percent increase in expenditures in the last five years! Crime went down in the 1990s by 50 percent or more, so the political elite might be considering reducing the expenditures on law and order by 50 percent. So a proposal for reallocating 10 percent is eminently reasonable, particularly as my estimates suggest that it will provide even larger reductions in victimization.

Less Law, More Order will help the political elite who want to reduce victimization deliberately and courageously while also reducing taxes. It provides the concrete steps to get a better investment in prevention that will yield real dividends by reducing the number of victims of crime and violence significantly and in a sustainable way. Each step is necessary and essential. Investment in successful prevention does not come from talk, hope, volunteers, or prizes—however laudable. It comes from policymakers investing real money, creating actual jobs, and passing laws to create a permanent Office for Crime Prevention. It comes from an intelligent and informed business plan and only 10 percent of all those reactive funds diverted to the reforms that make prevention and universal support and justice for victims a reality.

Less Law, More Order is hopeful because the evidence on what risk factors predispose young persons to become persistent offenders is so strong. The evaluations of innovative projects that tackle those risk factors prove that prevention works. Violence against women has been reduced and so can be prevented more. Fatalities on the road, abuse of alcohol, and illicit drugs have been reduced successfully. Crime has been reduced by changes in the design of community living and property. Police services have become more problem-oriented across cities and have reduced victimization in many neighborhoods. European and other governments are supporting victims more and even giving them a role to defend their search for truth, restitution, and their personal safety. Cities that take up the challenge to be tough on the risk factors that cause crime can demonstrate success.

Americans are paying twice as much as their Canadian and European counterparts for police, prisoners, and judges. Yet they still have much higher rates of fatal violence—five or six times higher. Imagine where Americans would be today if they took just $20 billion from that extra $100 billion a year more than their counterparts and spent it on the actionable recommendations discussed in this book. Imagine where the United States could be in ten years, if the U.S. Congress introduced a Crime Bill consistent with my proposals to multiply the use of effective crime prevention measures by the state and local governments. Imagine 100,000 more public health, youth, female counselors, and victim support professionals working on effective crime prevention strategies as well as police and judges being smarter in tackling the risk factors.

It is for policymakers to deliver what the public wants—less crime and more caring for victims. It is for policymakers to use our taxes in the most sustainable and cost-effective manner. Let's get smart and leave our children with fewer scars from violence within the home, with safer streets, and with a more sustainable way to deal with crime before it happens. Let's enshrine caring for victims in our culture and constitutions. Let's use truth and good sense to invest in proven prevention that invests in futures for young people, women, and all of us. The time to start was five years ago. In five years time, we will realize that the time to start was now. Invest in less law and more order now.

Notes

INTRODUCTION

1. Bureau of Justice Statistics, Criminal Victimization, 2004, 1.
2. Bureau of Justice Statistics, Justice Expenditure and Employment in the United States, 2003, 1, reported $185 billion for 2.4 million employees.
3. Bureau of Justice Statistics, Corrections Facts at a Glance, http://www.ojp.usdoj.gov/bjs/glance/, January 2006.
4. National Research Council (U.S.), *Fairness and Effectiveness in Policing*, 2004; Centers for Disease Control, Division of Violence Prevention, 2006; Audit Commission, *Misspent Youth*, 1996.
5. Bureau of Justice Statistics, *Sourcebook on Criminal Justice Statistics*, 31st edn, www.albany.edu/sourcebook, 2006.
6. Bureau of Justice Statistics, Justice Expenditure and Employment in the United States, 2001.
7. International Centre for Prevention of Crime, *Crime Prevention Digest II*, 1999; *100 Crime Prevention Programs*, 1999; *Urban Crime Prevention and Youth at Risk*, 2005.
8. Audit Commission, *Misspent Youth*, 1996.
9. National Criminal Justice Commission (U.S.), *The Real War on Crime*, 1996.
10. www.colorado.edu/cspv/blueprints/; ncjrs.org/html/ojjdp/jjbul2001_7_3/.
11. Sherman et al., *Evidence Based Crime Prevention*, 2002.
12. National Research Council (U.S.), *Fairness and Effectiveness in Policing*, 2004; National Research Council (U.S.), *Deadly Lessons*, 2003; National Research Council (U.S.), *Juvenile Crime, Juvenile Justice*, 2001; National Research Council (U.S.), *Informing America's Policy on Illegal Drugs*, 2001; National Research Council and Institute of Medicine, *Violence in Families*, 1998.

13. World Health Organization, World Report on Road Traffic Injury Prevention, 2004; World Health Organization, Preventing Violence, 2004; World Health Organization, World Report on Violence and Health, 2002.

14. Welsh and Farrington, *Preventing Crime*, 2006.

15. National Research Council (U.S.), *Fairness and Effectiveness in Policing*, 2004, 58.

16. Waller, *Men Released from Prison*, 1974; Home Office, *Reducing Offending*, 1998; Sherman et al., *Evidence Based Crime Prevention*, 2002, 330–403.

17. Zimring, *Perspectives on Deterrence*, 1971, 13–18.

18. Walmsley, *World Prison Population List*, 2004; Waller and Chan, *Prison Use*, 1977.

19. United States, President's Task Force on Victims of Crime, 1982.

20. United Nations General Assembly, Declaration of Basic Principles of Justice for Victims of Crime and Abuse of Power, 1985.

21. U.S. Office for Victims of Crime, *New Directions from the Field*, 1998.

CHAPTER 1

1. Bureau of Justice Statistics, Justice Expenditure and Employment in the United States, 2001.

2. In 2004, BJS reported 800,000 sworn police officers, which is a 73 percent rise.

3. Waller and Chan, *Prison Use*, 1977.

4. Most of those increases occurred after violent crime was dropping. That is, the less the violent crime, the more expenditures increased—not the reverse. We will see that the best estimates are that 27 percent of the overall reduction in crime can be ascribed to the 300 percent increase in inmates. See Spelman in Blumstein and Wallman, *The Crime Drop in America*, 2000, 123.

5. United States. President's Commission on Law Enforcement and Administration of Justice, 1968.

6. National Research Council, *Fairness and Effectiveness in Policing*, 2004.

7. Her Majesty's Inspectorate of Constabulary, *Beating Crime*, 1998.

8. Waller, *Men Released from Prison*, 1974.

9. Spelman in Blumstein and Wallman, *The Crime Drop in America*, 2000, 97–125.

10. Home Office, *Digest 4*, 1999, 29.

11. See International Centre for Prevention of Crime, *100 Crime Prevention Programs*, 1999.

12. The conclusions from these conferences are available in International Centre for Prevention of Crime, *Crime Prevention Digest II*, 1999.

13. See, for instance, Waller and Sansfaçon, *Investing Wisely in Prevention*, 2000.

14. Audit Commission, *Misspent Youth*, 1996.

15. Home Office, *Reducing Offending*, 1998.

16. www.colorado.edu/cspv/blueprints/; ncjrs.org/html/ojjdp/jjbul2001_7_3/.

17. Sherman et al., *Evidence Based Crime Prevention*, 2002.

18. Sarre, *Beyond what works?* 2001.

19. World Health Organization, World Report on Violence and Health, 2002; World Health Organization, World Report on Road Traffic Injury Prevention, 2004.

CHAPTER 2

1. National Research Council (U.S.), *Juvenile Crime, Juvenile Justice*, 2001, 3–4 and 66–104.

2. National Research Council (U.S.), *Juvenile Crime, Juvenile Justice*, 2001, 3–4.

3. International Centre for Prevention of Crime, *Crime Prevention Digest II*, 1999; National Research Council (U.S.), *Juvenile Crime, Juvenile Justice*, 2001.

4. National Research Council (U.S.), *Juvenile Crime, Juvenile Justice*, 2001.

5. Schweinhart, *The High/Scope Perry Preschool Study through Age 40*, 2005.

6. Elliott, Blue Prints for Violence Prevention, 2005, www.colorado.edu/cspv/blueprints.

7. National Association of Attorneys General, Bruised Inside, 2000.

8. Sherman et al. *Evidence Based Crime Prevention*, 2002, 215–217 and 232.

9. McConnell, National Job Corps Study, 2001.

10. Blumstein and Wallman, *The Crime Drop in America*, 2000, 9–10.

11. Karmen, *New York Murder Mystery*, 2000, 194–216 and 265.

12. International Centre for Prevention of Crime, *Crime Prevention Digest II*, 1999.

CHAPTER 3

1. World Health Organization, *World Report on Violence and Health*, 2004.

2. World Health Organization, *World Report on Road Traffic Injury Prevention*, 2004.

3. National Research Council and Institute of Medicine, *Violence in Families*, 1998, 4–5; World Health Organization, *World Report on Violence and Health*, 2004.

4. National Research Council and Institute of Medicine, *Violence in Families*, 1998.

5. Dugan, *Explaining the Decline in Intimate Partner Homicide*, 1999, 187–214.

6. Sloan et al., Handgun Regulations, Crime, Assaults and Homicide, 1988.

7. Carroll, Gun Ownership and Use in America, *The Gallup Poll*, 22 November 2005.

8. Sherman et al., *Evidence Based Crime Prevention*, 2002, 187–189.

9. National Research Council (U.S.), *Fairness and Effectiveness in Policing*, 2004, 239.

10. Blumstein and Wallman, *The Crime Drop in America*, 2000, 10–11.

11. Willett, *Criminal on the Road*, 1971.

12. Karmen, *New York Murder Mystery*, 2000, 185–187 and 265.

13. Sherman et al., *Evidence Based Crime Prevention*, 2002

14. http://www.city.vancouver.bc.ca/fourpillars/, January 2006.

15. Elliott, Blue Prints for Violence Prevention, 2005, www.colorado.edu/cspv/blueprints.

CHAPTER 4

1. Waller and Okihiro, *Burglary, the Victim and the Public*, 1978.

2. Sherman et al., *Evidence Based Crime Prevention*, 2002.

3. National Research Council (U.S.), *Fairness and Effectiveness in Policing*, 2004, 246–251.

4. Waller, *What Reduces Residential Burglary?* 1982.

5. Sherman et al., *Evidence Based Crime Prevention*, 2002, 315–321.

6. Farrell and Pease in Welsh and Farrington, *Preventing Crime*, 2006, 162–176.

7. Waller and Okihiro, *Burglary, the Victim and the Public*, 1978.

8. Hurley and Earls, *On Crime as Science*, 2004.

9. Welsh and Farrington, *Preventing Crime*, 2006, 193–207.

10. Clarke, *Situational Crime Prevention*, 1997.

11. Welsh and Farrington, *Preventing Crime*, 2006, 209–225.

CHAPTER 5

1. National Research Council (U.S.), *Fairness and Effectiveness in Policing*, 2004, 58.

2. National Research Council (U.S.), *Fairness and Effectiveness in Policing*, 2004, 224–225.

3. National Research Council (U.S.), *Fairness and Effectiveness in Policing*, 2004, 4–5.

4. Her Majesty's Inspectorate of Constabulary, *Beating Crime*, 1998.

5. Welsh and Farrington, *Preventing Crime*, 2006, 1.

6. Center for Problem Oriented Policing—www.popcenter.org.

7. Karmen, *New York Murder Mystery*, 2000, xi–xiii.

8. Bureau of Justice Statistics, Crime and Victimization in the Three Largest Metropolitan Areas, 2005.

9. Kelling and Sousa, *Do Police Matter?* 2001.

10. Karmen, *New York Murder Mystery*, 2000.

11. National Crime Prevention Council (U.S.), *Six Safer Cities*, 1999.

12. Wilson and Kelling, Broken Windows, 1982.

13. Kelling and Sousa, *Do Police Matter?* 2001.

14. Zimring, *Perspectives on Deterrence*, 1971.

15. National Research Council (U.S.), *Fairness and Effectiveness in Policing*, 2004, 217–250; Sherman et al., *Evidence Based Crime Prevention*, 2002, 295–329; Blumstein and Wallman, *The Crime Drop in America*, 2000, 207–265.

16. Kelling and Sousa, *Do Police Matter?* 2001, F.N. 22.

17. National Crime Prevention Council (U.S.), *Six Safer Cities*, 1999.

18. Kennedy et al., *Reducing Gun Violence*, 2001.

19. Skogan and Hartnett, *Community Policing*, 1997, 219–230 and 242–244.

20. Bureau of Justice Statistics, Crime and Victimization in the Three Largest Metropolitan Areas, 1980–98, 2005.

CHAPTER 6

1. Waller, *Crime Victims*, 2003; United Nations General Assembly, Declaration of Basic Principles of Justice for Victims, 1985.

2. United States, President's Task Force on Victims of Crime, 1982.

3. Bureau of Justice Statistics, Criminal Victimization, 2004.

4. General Assembly resolution 40/34 of 29 November 1985, which adopted the Declaration of Basic Principles of Justice for Victims, 1985.

5. United Nations General Assembly, Declaration of Basic Principles of Justice for Victims, 1985.

6. Bureau of Justice Statistics, Criminal Victimization, 2004.

7. Waller in Lurigio, Skogan, and Davis, *Victims of Crime*, 1st edn, 1990, 139–156.

8. Doe, *The Story of Jane Doe*, 2004.

9. U.S. Office for Victims of Crime, *New Directions from the Field*, 1998.

10. Strang and Sherman in Welsh and Farrington, *Preventing Crime*, 2006, 147–160.

11. Part 1 of H.R. 5107, 20 January 2004.

12. Rome Statute of the International Criminal Court, 1998.

CHAPTER 7

1. International Centre for Prevention of Crime, *Crime Prevention Digest II*, 1999.

2. See International Centre for Prevention of Crime, *Crime Prevention Digest II*, 1999, 51–70.

3. National Institute of Justice, National Evaluation of Weed and Seed, 1999.

4. Acero Velásquez, The City and Public Policies, 2003.

5. International Centre for Prevention of Crime, *Crime Prevention Digest II*, 1999.

CHAPTER 8

1. U.S. Office for Victims of Crime, *New Directions from the Field*, 1998.

CHAPTER 9

1. Sourcebook of Criminal Justice Statistics Online, www.albany.edu/sourcebook/wk1/t228.wk1.

Principal Sources

Acero Velásquez, Hugo. "The City and Public Policies on Safety and Congruous Living." Private communication from City Hall, Bogotá, 2003.

Audit Commission. *Misspent Youth: Young People and Crime*. London: Audit Commission for Local Authorities and National Health Service in England and Wales, 1996.

Blumstein, Al, and J. Wallman, eds. *The Crime Drop in America*. Cambridge: Cambridge University Press, 2000.

Bureau of Justice Statistics. Crime and Victimization in the Three Largest Metropolitan Areas, 1980–98. Washington, DC: U.S. Department of Justice, 2005.

Bureau of Justice Statistics. Criminal Victimization, 2004. Washington, DC: U.S. Department of Justice, 2005.

Bureau of Justice Statistics. Justice Expenditure and Employment in the United States, 2001. Washington, DC: U.S. Department of Justice, 2004.

Bureau of Justice Statistics. *Sourcebook on Criminal Justice Statistics*, 31st edn, 2006. Available at www.albany.edu/sourcebook.

Carroll, Joseph. Gun Ownership and Use in America. Women More Likely Than Men to Use Guns for Protection. *The Gallup Poll*, 22 November 2005.

Centers for Disease Control, Division of Violence Prevention, National Center for Injury Prevention and Control, 2006. Available at www.cdc.gov/ncipc/dvp.

Clarke, Ronald. *Situational Crime Prevention: Successful Case Studies*. Albany, NY: Harrow and Heston, 1997.

Doe, Jane. *The Story of Jane Doe: A Book about Rape*. Toronto: Vintage Canada, 2004.

Dugan, Laura, Daniel Nagin, and Richard Rosenfeld. "Explaining the Decline in Intimate Partner Homicide: The Effects of Changing Domesticity, Women's Status, and Domestic Violence Resources." *Homicide Studies*, 3(3): 187–214, August 1999.

Elliott, Delbert. Blue Prints for Violence Prevention, 2005. Available at http://www.colorado.edu/cspv/blueprints.

Her Majesty's Inspectorate of Constabulary. *Beating Crime*. London: Home Office, 1998.

Home Office. *Digest 4: Information on the Criminal Justice System in England and Wales*, London: Home Office, 1999.

Home Office. *Reducing Offending: An Assessment of Research Evidence on Ways of Dealing with Offending Behaviour*, Peter Goldblatt and Chris Lewis, eds. London: Home Office, Research and Statistics, 1998.

Hurley, Dan, and Felton Earls. "On Crime as Science (A Neighbor at a Time)." *New York Times*, 6 January 2004.

International Centre for Prevention of Crime. *Urban Crime Prevention and Youth at Risk: Compendium of Promising Strategies and Programs from Around the World*. Montreal, 2005.

International Centre for Prevention of Crime. *Crime Prevention Digest II: Comparative Analysis of Successful Community Safety*. Montreal, 1999.

International Centre for Prevention of Crime. *100 Crime Prevention Programs to Inspire Action Across the World*. Montreal, 1999.

Karmen, Andrew. *New York Murder Mystery: The True Story Behind the Crime Crash of the 1990s*. New York: New York University Press, 2000.

Kelling, George, and William Sousa. *Do Police Matter? An Analysis of the Impact of New York City's Police Reforms*. New York: Center for Civic Innovation at the Manhattan Institute, Civic Report, December 2001.

Kelling, George, Tony Pate, Duane Dieckman, and Charles Brown. *Kansas City Preventive Patrol Experiment: A Summary Report*. Washington, DC: Police Foundation, 1974.

Kennedy, David, Anthony Braga, Anne Piehl, and Elin Waring. *Reducing Gun Violence: The Boston Gun Project's Operation Ceasefire*. Washington, DC: U.S. Department of Justice, National Institute of Justice, 2001.

McConnell, Sheena, and Steven Glazerman. National Job Corps Study: The Benefits and Costs of Job Corps. Princeton, NJ: Mathematica Policy Research, Inc., June 2001.

National Association of Attorneys General. Bruised Inside: What Our Children Say about Youth Violence, What Causes it, and What We Need to do about it. A Report of the National Association of Attorneys General, 2002.

National Crime Prevention Council (U.S.). *Six Safer Cities: On the Crest of the Crime Prevention Wave*. Washington, DC, 1999.

National Criminal Justice Commission (U.S.). *The Real War on Crime: The Report of the National Criminal Justice Commission*, Steven Donziger, ed. New York: Harper, 1996.

National Research Council (U.S.). *Fairness and Effectiveness in Policing: The Evidence*, Wesley Skogan, ed. Washington, DC: National Academies Press, 2004.

National Research Council (U.S.). *Deadly Lessons: Understanding Lethal School Violence*, Mark Moore, Carol Petrie, Anthony Braga, and Brenda McLaughlin, eds. Washington, DC: National Academy Press, 2003.

National Research Council (U.S.). *Juvenile Crime, Juvenile Justice*, Joan McCord, Cathy Spatz Widom, and Nancy Crowell, eds. Washington, DC: National Academy Press, 2001.

National Research Council (U.S.). *Informing America's Policy on Illegal Drugs: What We Don't Know Keeps Hurting Us*, Committee on Data and Research for Policy on Illegal Drugs, Charles Manski, John Pepper, Carol Petrie, and Brenda McLaughlin, eds. Washington, DC: National Academy Press, 2001.

National Research Council and Institute of Medicine. *Violence in Families: Assessing Prevention and Treatment Programs*. Committee on the Assessment of Family Violence Interventions, Board on Children, Youth, and Families, Rosemary Chalk and Patricia King, eds. Washington, DC: National Academy Press, 1998.

Rome Statute of the International Criminal Court, United Nations Conference of Plenipotentiaries on the Establishment of an International Criminal Court A/Conf.183/9. New York: United Nations, 1998.

Saad, Lydia. "Wanted in Great Britain: Law and Order." *The Gallup Poll*, 24 February 2004.

Sarre, R. Beyond "'What Works?': A 25 Year Jubilee Retrospective of Robert Martinson's Famous Article." *The Australian and New Zealand Journal of Criminology*, 34(1): 38–46, 2001.

Schweinhart, Lawrence. *The High/Scope Perry Preschool Study through Age 40: Summary, Conclusions and Frequently Asked Questions*. Ypsilanti, MI: High/Scope Press, 2005.

Sherman, Lawrence, David Farrington, Brandon Welsh, and Doris MacKenzie. *Evidence Based Crime Prevention*. New York: Routledge, 2002.

Skogan, Wesley, and Susan Hartnett. *Community Policing: Chicago Style*. New York: Oxford University Press, 1997.

Sloan, J.H., A.L. Kellerman, D.T. Reay, J.A. Ferris, T. Koepsell, F.P. Rivara et al. "Handgun Regulations, Crime, Assaults and Homicide: A Tale of Two Cities." *New England Journal of Medicine*, 319: 1256–1262, 1988.

United Nations General Assembly. Declaration of Basic Principles of Justice for Victims of Crime and Abuse of Power. New York, 1985. Available at www.unhchr.ch/html/intlinst.htm.

United Nations, Economic and Social Council. Guidelines for the Prevention of Crime in Action to Promote Effective Crime Prevention. New York: United Nations, Economic and Social Council, Office for Drug Control and Crime Prevention, 2002.

United States. President's Task Force on Victims of Crime: Final Report. Washington, DC, 1982.

United States. President's Commission on Law Enforcement and Administration of Justice. New York: Avon, 1968.

U.S. Office for Victims of Crime. *New Directions from the Field: Victims' Rights and Services for the 21st Century*. Washington, DC: U.S. Department of Justice, Office of Justice Programs, 1998.

Waller, Irvin. *Crime Victims: Doing Justice to Their Support and Protection*. Helsinki: European Institute for Crime Prevention and Control, 2003.

Waller, Irvin, and Daniel Sansfaçon. *Investing Wisely in Prevention: International Experiences*. Monograph, Crime Prevention Series #1. Washington, DC: U.S. Department of Justice, Bureau of Justice Assistance, 2000.

Waller, Irvin. "The Police: 'First in Aid'." In *Victims of Crime: Problems, Policies, and Programs*, 1st edn., Arthur Lurigio, W.G. Skogan, and R.C. Davis, eds. Newbury Park, CA: Sage, 1990, pp. 139–156.

Waller, Irvin. "What Reduces Residential Burglary: Action and Research in Seattle and Toronto." In *The Victim in International Perspective*, Hans Joachim Schneider, ed. New York: De Gruyter, 1982, pp. 479–492.

Waller, Irvin, and Norm Okihiro. *Burglary, the Victim and the Public*. Toronto: University of Toronto Press, 1978.

Waller, Irvin, and Janet Chan. "Prison Use: A Canadian and International Comparison." In *Correctional Institutions*, 2nd edn., L.T. Wilkins and D. Glazer, eds. J.B. Lippincott, Philadelphia, PA, 1977, pp. 41–60.

Waller, Irvin. *Men Released from Prison*. Toronto: University of Toronto Press, 1974.

Walmsley, Roy. *World Prison Population List*, 5th edn. Research Findings, 234. London: Home Office Research, 2004.

Welsh, Brandon, and David Farrington, eds. *Preventing Crime: What Works for Children, Offenders, Victims, and Places*. New York: Springer, 2006.

Willett, Terrence. *Criminal on the Road, a Study of Serious Motoring Offences and Those Who Commit Them*. London: Tavistock, 1971.

Wilson, James, and George Kelling. "Broken Windows: The Police and Neighborhood Safety." *Atlantic Monthly*, 29–38, March 1982.

World Health Organization World Report on Road Traffic Injury Prevention: Summary. Geneva, 2004.

World Health Organization. Preventing Violence: A Guide to Implementing the Recommendations of the World Report on Violence and Health. Geneva: Violence and Injuries Prevention, 2004.

World Health Organization. World Report on Violence and Health. Geneva: Violence and Injuries Prevention, 2002.

Zimring, Franklin. *Perspectives on Deterrence*. Chicago: Chicago University Press, 1971.

Index

About the Author

IRVIN WALLER is Professor of Criminology at Univesity of Ottawa. He is the founding CEO of the International Centre for Prevention of Crime in Montreal. He is the author of *Men Released from Prison* and *Burglary: The Victim and the Public*. His most recent work has been in researching and writing policy pamphlets for organizations such as the U.S. Department of Justice, the Canadian Council for Social Development, the Soros Foundation, and the UN European Institute on Crime Prevention and Criminal Justice.